The Praxis of Christian Experience

*An Introduction
to the Theology
of Edward Schillebeeckx*

Robert J. Schreiter, C.PP.S.
Mary Catherine Hilkert, O.P.

1817

Harper & Row, Publishers, San Francisco

New York, Cambridge, Philadelphia, St. Louis
London, Singapore, Sydney, Tokyo

THE PRAXIS OF CHRISTIAN EXPERIENCE: AN INTRODUCTION TO THE THEOLOGY OF EDWARD SCHILLEBEECKX. Copyright ©1989 by Robert Schreiter and Catherine Hilkert. All rights reserved. Printed in the United States of America. No part of this book may be used or reproduced in any manner whatsoever without written permission except in the case of brief quotations embodied in critical articles and reviews. For information address Harper & Row, Publishers, Inc., 10 East 53rd Street, New York, NY 10022. Published simultaneously in Canada by Fitzhenry & Whiteside, Limited, Toronto.

FIRST EDITION

Library of Congress Cataloging-in-Publication Data

The Praxis of Christian experience.

    "Works of Edward Schillebeeckx cited": p.
    Includes index.
    1. Schillebeeckx, Edward, 1914–
I. Schreiter, Robert J.   II. Hilkert, Mary Catherine.
BX4705.S51314P73   1989   230'.2'0924   88–45688
ISBN 0–06–067137–8

89 90 91 92 93 RRD 10 9 8 7 6 5 4 3 2 1

Contents

Introduction

Edward Schillebeeckx once remarked that "a theologian can wish no more than to bring people, even believers in crisis, to the point of saying 'yes' to the heart of the gospel" (*Interim Report*, p. 39). The pastoral concern that has motivated and permeated Schillebeeckx's theological work over the past forty years has emerged even more clearly in his recent efforts to rethink the story of Jesus (*Jesus: An Experiment in Christology*) and the Christian experience of salvation (*Christ: The Experience of Jesus as Lord*) in the face of the history of human suffering and the growing crisis of credibility confronting the Christian faith. Similarly, his recent investigations of the development of the church's ministerial structures and theology (*Ministry: Leadership in the Community of Jesus Christ* and *The Church with a Human Face*) were prompted by concrete pastoral situations of crisis and conflict centering around the increasing shortage of ordained ministers, the number of local communities deprived of Eucharist, and the emerging forms of alternative practice in local communities of faith.

Schillebeeckx's theological vision has developed in response to the needs and experience of contemporary believers and those who would seek to believe. He has tried to make serious academic theology available to "the ordinary Christian" and has said that he is even willing to consign his books to the sale rack of a curio shop if they fail to contribute to the recovery of a living faith in our day. However, his work is not always easily accessible due to the length of his books, the breadth and detail of the scholarly research he includes, and the inevitably technical theological language that the depth of his thought demands.

Still his theological project has caught the imagination of many in the North American audience—as elsewhere in the world— who are seeking to discover whether it is possible to believe in our day, as Schillebeeckx boldly claims, that "compassion is at the heart of reality" and that Jesus is God's "no" to human suffering. Students, catechists, pastoral ministers, study groups, ecumenical audiences, and other interested adults who have had some initial exposure to Schillebeeckx's theology often ask where to begin in trying to understand his thought more deeply.

How, then, might they do this? The popular interview *God Is New Each Moment* offers a sample of some of Schillebeeckx's provocative insights, but the genre of an interview precludes the kind of context, development, and nuance of thought necessary to do justice to the complexity and richness of Schillebeeckx's thinking. *God Among Us: The Gospel Proclaimed,* a collection of Schillebeeckx's homilies and lectures in spirituality, provides more adequate access to the most basic and recurring themes in Schillebeeckx's contemporary writings, but those very themes are more easily recognized by one who is already familiar with Schillebeeckx's theology. The *Interim Report on the Books "Jesus" and "Christ"* includes a summary and clarification of some of the significant issues in Schillebeeckx's two volumes in christology, but the book was written as a response to his critics rather than as a synthesis of his christology; hence the main lines of development are not always clear and major sections are omitted. *The Schillebeeckx Reader* presents focal texts from Schillebeeckx's major writings over the course of his career and provides valuable previously untranslated sources. While a general orientation to Schillebeeckx's thought and a brief commentary at the beginning of each section help to situate the excerpts, the purpose of the *Reader* is to provide direct access to Schillebeeckx's writings rather than to present an exposition of his thought for a broader audience.

In contrast to those works, this volume is intended to provide a general introduction to Schillebeeckx's contemporary writings, specifically to the major theological themes explored in his two-volume christology, *Jesus* and *Christ,* and in his two ministry books. The primary focus of the book is a clear exposition of Schillebeeckx's contemporary theological positions rather than the historical development of his thought or theological critique of his views, though the latter concerns are included in several of the chapters.

While Schillebeeckx has not fashioned an overall systematic theology (and questions whether that is even possible in an age that takes seriously the ambiguity of history and the absurdity of evil and suffering), the scope of his research and thinking extends well beyond the focal areas of christology/soteriology and ministry. Major themes from his earlier works—revelation and theology, church and sacraments, hermeneutics and method, eschatology, ethics, and Christian spirituality—reemerge in new contexts and perspectives in his recent books, as the selection of chapter topics for this work suggests. Neither the selection of themes nor the exposition in any individual chapter claims to be exhaustive. Rather this volume offers an introduction to major aspects of Schillebeeckx's theology and is intended to lead readers back to Schillebeeckx's own writings. For that reason, suggestions for further reading are provided at the end of each chapter. The glossaries at the end of *Jesus* and *Christ* (entitled "Technical Information") may also prove helpful to serious students of Schillebeeckx's thought.

OVERVIEW OF THIS VOLUME

In the opening chapter William Hill offers an overview of Schillebeeckx's "theology in transition," highlighting a primary theme in Schillebeeckx's work that recurs throughout the succeeding chapters: God's cause is the human cause. Reviewing Schillebeeckx's personal history and the roots of his theological development from his Thomist origins through the influence of phenomenology and hermeneutics to his recent understanding of theology as a critical and political task, Hill calls attention to an underlying (Thomistic) conviction that pervades Schillebeeckx's varied writings: the absolute primacy of God and God's grace in history. Hill's chapter functions as something of an overture for the rest of the book, suggesting leitmotifs that are developed in further detail in the chapters that follow. For that reason readers may wish to return to the opening chapter after completing the book.

Developing the broad lines of Schillebeeckx's theological method outlined by Hill, William Portier in the second chapter situates Schillebeeckx's approach to the theological task in terms of both contemporary North American concern with theological method and the Dutch Catholic context in which his theology was born. Portier underlines the necessity of theology's commitment to a historical praxis of mysticism and politics (another theme that recurs in later chapters) and concludes that Schillebeeckx has "reconceived theology as a form of reflection with intimate bonds to Christian living." Because, as Portier notes, discussion of method in theology emerges only from reflection on the actual practice of the theological task, Portier's chapter, like Hill's, can be profitably reread after reading the other chapters.

At the base of Schillebeeckx's contemporary theological reflection is the conviction that revelation occurs in history; traces of the living God can be discovered in human experience, even in the experience of radical suffering. Drawing on untranslated sources that expand the initial discussion of revelation and experience in Schillebeeckx's *Christ* and the brief treatments of the topic in *Jesus* and *Interim Report,* Mary Catherine Hilkert examines in Chapter 3 the interwoven threads that constitute Schillebeeckx's claim that revelation occurs in, but is not identical with, human experience: the revelatory structure of human experience, the necessity of a faith horizon for the religious experience of revelation, the Christian claim that God has been revealed uniquely in Jesus, and the historical transmission of the experience of revelation through a living tradition of faith.

Chapters 4 and 5 present the soteriological christology that has been at the center of Schillebeeckx's recent theological efforts. Locating Schillebeeckx within the broader discussion in contemporary christology, John Galvin emphasizes the uniqueness of Schillebeeckx's option for a narrative christology forged in the face of human suffering. Noting the breadth of Schillebeeckx's exegetical research, Galvin traces the main outlines of the *Jesus* book, highlighting the features of the "historical Jesus" that led to the later Christian confession of christological faith. Following a careful analysis of Schillebeeckx's unique interpretation of the death and resurrection of Jesus and his discussion of the development of early Christian plural strands of faith, Galvin raises important critical questions regarding Schillebeeckx's christology.

The soteriological focus of Schillebeeckx's christology is developed further by Janet Callewaert in Chapter 5. Callewaert explains how Schillebeeckx's move toward a contemporary soteriology in Part IV of the *Christ* volume is carefully interrelated with both the christology of *Jesus* and the analysis of New Testament understandings of salvation that constitute the major portion of the *Christ* volume. After a brief overview of Schillebeeckx's theological synthesis of New Testament theologies of grace and his outline of the four structural elements that must undergird any current soteriology, the chapter concentrates on Schillebeeckx's analysis of the contemporary historical situation characterized by massive human suffering as the context for any contemporary soteriology and the problem of the relationship between human efforts towards self-liberation and the promise of final redemption by God.

Underlying both the christology and the ministry books is a profound Christian spirituality rooted in Jesus' "*Abba* experience" and the conviction that the Holy Spirit is the source and guide of the living Christian tradition. Donald Goergen, in Chapter 6, shows the roots of Schillebeeckx's spirituality in the heritage of his Dominican tradition, which stresses a twofold "presence to God" and "presence to the world." Locating the foundation of Schillebeeckx's spirituality in Jesus as "parable of God" and "paradigm of humanity," Goergen shows how the "following of Jesus" involves a "praxis of the reign of God" that is at once mystical and political.

The unity of the divine and the human that is at the core of Schillebeeckx's spirituality is also central to his developing theology of church and sacraments, a theme Susan Ross demonstrates in Chapter 7. Following the development in Schillebeeckx's thought from his groundbreaking *Christ the Sacrament of the Encounter with God* (1963) through his recent writings influenced by critical theory, Ross detects a profound continuity in Schillebeeckx's focus on the concrete and historical dimensions of life as the locus of God's revelation. From that perspective she shows how Schillebeeckx's theology of church as sacrament of salvation now incorporates critical analysis of the concrete historical development of the church and the emerging role of critical local communities. Further, Ross explains how Schillebeeckx's early theology of the sacraments as "encounters with God" remains significant in his present discussion of sacraments as anticipatory signs.

Schillebeeckx's sacramental understanding of church, when combined with his critical analysis of the historical development of ecclesial office, has serious implications for his theology of ministry, as Mary Hines illustrates in Chapter 8. Tracing the main lines of *The Church with a Human Face,* Hines shows how the book serves as an excellent example of Schillebeeckx's theological method, which calls for a mutually critical correlation of present Christian experience and the past history of "the great Christian tradition." Noting that, according to Schillebeeckx, the various cultural manifestations of ministry that have evolved throughout the church's history are "legitimate but not necessary" responses to various social and theological situations, Hines explains how, for Schillebeeckx, the present crisis of ordained leadership exists because of a failure to understand the implications of the sacramental nature of the church as the place where the Spirit dwells.

In Chapter 9 Bradford Hinze discusses the interrelationship of eschatology and ethics, two major concerns in Schillebeeckx's recent theological work. Hinze observes that Schillebeeckx's constant concern with history as the arena for human encounter with God has shifted in relation to the development of his understanding of Jesus as "eschatological prophet" and his increasing awareness of the dimensions of human suffering and oppression at the present moment in history. The move from a sacramental eschatology rooted in the incarnation to a truly prophetic vision of history transforms both human expectations of salvation and the ethics demanded of disciples. Noting that Schillebeeckx considers any ethical model—whether from the New Testament or the later Christian tradition—to be socially and historically conditioned, Hinze explains Schillebeeckx's understanding of the importance and function for Christian ethics of the biblical narrative, which presents a distinct eschatological ethic grounded in the life and teachings of Jesus.

In a final chapter, Robert Schreiter probes some of the foundational aspects of Schillebeeckx's thought, exploring especially some of those things that contribute to his enduring influence, especially among his North American and First World readership today. He identifies four such commitments in his writing: a commitment to working inductively rather deductively; a commitment to the narrative character of experience; a concern for the mystery of suffering and the contrast experience; and a commitment to the primacy of soteriology in the christological project.

He indicates how some of these themes surfaced time and again in the contributions to this volume.

It is hoped that this introduction to the thought of an important theologian will be useful to those encountering Schillebeeckx's thought for the first time as well as to those who are already familiar with his work.

The Editors

1. Human Happiness as God's Honor: Background to a Theology in Transition

WILLIAM J. HILL, O.P.

FOREGROUND: THEOLOGY IN A NEW KEY

It has been said that the question of God is not one question among the others or even the most important of the questions, but the only question there is (S. Ogden). In the waning years of the twentieth century, this translates into the question of whether it is possible to believe any longer in the God of Christianity. Perhaps it is truer to see this as a crisis not of faith itself, but of culture. What is taken for granted in an age of secularity is not the demise of God in his own reality but of the cultural mediations of God. The latter, it is felt, have become archaic and "ideological"; they are obtrusions of abstract ideas upon reality that in effect distort life as we know it, offering to believers notions of God that are alienating and in truth sub-Christian. The agonizing question that unavoidably urges itself upon us is: are we on the verge of ceasing to believe? Or have we come to the point where at last we are capable of becoming believers in an authentic sense? The frightening problem that can only be faced honestly is that of the credibility of Catholicism in the contemporary world. It is this question that has centrally engaged the theological work of Edward Schillebeeckx, a lifetime engagement the critical force of which has not been compromised by the personal intensity he brings to the project.

That faith in God is possible—even necessary in the sense that human existence has no ultimate meaning without God—pivots on whether we truly believe and trust in the human as that which has been made one with God in Christ. Everything turns on acknowledging the truth of the incarnation (i.e., of the hypostatic union Schillebeeckx prefers to call a hypostatic unity); namely, that the human as such is part of the object of faith insofar as God has, in his unexacted love, made "the human cause to be his [God's] cause." This is an uninhibited confirmation of the human as such and as the locus of God's revelatory act, which latter thus acquires an experiential and self-authenticating character. It is in the immediacy of human experience that the transcendent is mediated to us, experience at once individual and social, i.e., both personal and historically intersubjective. The Christian doctrines of creation and incarnation mean, respectively, that God does not wish to be everything in an exclusive sense and that he wishes to be actively present to and involved in human affairs. Thus, one cannot love God otherwise than by loving humanity, and loving humankind is not loving the individual in isolation but as he or she concretely lives within the structures of social existence. Christian love has thereby simultaneously a vertical (toward God) and a horizontal (toward humanity) dimension. Needless to say, none of this emphasis upon present experience as disclosive of God is meant to minimize the other indispensable pole to revelation; namely, the sacred Scriptures as the articulation in a normative way of the original and privileged experience of Jesus' disciples and the continued mediation and interpretation of that experience by way of the living tradition of the Christian church. Revelation is thus a dialectical act in which past and present converge without priority being afforded to either.

What is no longer possible in the modern world is to accept on no other basis than that of the unalloyed authority of others that God has drawn near to us in Christ. We can no longer abdicate our thinking to others irresponsibly without some touchstone for truth in our own experience. Secular experience in its very secularity must supply some "inner references toward an absolute mystery without which even secularity is threatened with collapse." Schillebeeckx himself has articulated this truth in a lucid phrase: "Christianity is not a message which has to be believed, but an experience of faith which becomes a message, and as an explicit message seeks to offer a new possibility of life experience to others who hear it from within their own experience" (*Interim*

Report, p. 50). What this makes clear is that all revelation from God occurs as experience; the full impact of that is furthered in the awareness that all experience in turn is interpreted experience. How such experience achieves a necessary universal character remains, of course, problematic. Schillebeeckx's explanation is that the universality is only that which is possible historically; i.e., we experience the same reality and events as did the first disciples—the experience of God proffering salvation in Christ— but in the context of our epoch rather than theirs. One difference, of course, is that they mediate our experience by what they have brought to language in the New Testament and what has been mediated further by living tradition. What is experienced in this interpreted way is not merely the message conveyed to us but, through that, the phenomenon of the Jesus movement itself. In our own vastly differing cultural context and interpretative framework, we do not merely seek for historical reconstruction but endeavor to experience for ourselves what the first disciples experienced. God's loving action toward contemporary humankind is, after all, not any less than it was toward those to whom it was first offered historically.

In an attempt to identify further the kind of interpreted experience that is in question here for believers, Schillebeeckx notes that it is more a matter of orthopraxis than of orthodoxy; it is more a matter of living out the truths and values of the gospel than of illuminating them theoretically. The Christian response to the gospel seeks (in a spirit akin to that of neo-Marxism) not just to explain the world in one more way, but to change it by bringing it into the kingdom of God. Without neglecting the past (which neglect would mean a total loss of identity) Christianity's present concern assigns priority to the future. Christian life practice cannot exist in isolation from theory, and without it would lack all criteria for truth. Still it is the more fundamental dimension of human existing from which theories are reflectively derived and is far more than the mere practical implementation of theory. Praxis means precisely this dialectical interacting of theory and concrete action.

There is, however, a dark specter that looms over this optimistic human posture. Christian praxis, which is by nature social and historical, finds itself confronted with overweening forces of evil and suffering, especially evil and suffering that are undeserved, that seemingly prevail in the end—unavoidably so in the case of death. Such negativity calls into question God's benign presence in the world. In the face of this consideration, some theologians have not hesitated to lay evil at God's door, making God at least its indirect cause in not precluding evil from the world. Others, wishing to absolve God of moral fault, have simply cast him in the role of a cosmic deity, finite in power and capable at the most of only mitigating the powers of evil that menace the world. Most influential at the moment, perhaps, is the position adopted by Jürgen Moltmann, for whom the origin of evil lies outside of God, but whose love nevertheless leads him to absorb it within himself (truly willing then to suffer in his very divinity) and in the process negating its power and drawing from it positive values. Schillebeeckx's thought, by contrast, takes a different tack, absolving God of all complicity in evil and rendering God ontologically impervious to any experience of it in virtue of his transcendence of all that is finite. The source of the evil that is human suffering lies with the finite and fallible freedom of humanity, which, in a memorable phrase of Yves Congar, possesses the one awesome power over God of being able to negate and shatter his loving initiatives. A classical expression of this view (though one that both Aquinas and Luther would find extreme) is to be found in the work of the fifteenth-century Italian humanist Pico della Mirandola, who has God say to humankind in the *Oration on the Dignity of Man:*

We have made you a creature neither of heaven nor of earth, neither mortal nor immortal, in order that you may, as the free and proud shaper of your own being, fashion yourself in the form you may prefer. It will be in your power to descend to the lower, brutish forms of life; you will be able, through your own decision, to rise again to the superior orders whose life is divine.

Undergirding this abuse of freedom, however, lies the finitude of the cosmos itself, which, held out in existence over the void by God, is by necessity prone to the intersecting of opposing causalities that unavoidably give rise to physical evil. At this point, evil becomes a surd the ultimate meaning or, perhaps better, the meaninglessness of which lies beyond our ken. With Wittgenstein, we must fall silent before that of which we cannot speak.

Robert Butterworth has astutely observed here that we have no profounder guide than the book of Job, which leaves the existence of evil as a mystery that gainsays all our efforts at explanation.

It has been a hallmark of Schillebeeckx's theology to proclaim the active presence and goodness of the transcendent against this all-pervasive phenomenon of evil and to do so in the very face of the dark and demonic forces modern humans have called to life—science, technology, industrialization, the circle of poverty, terrorism in the interest of self-aggrandizement, and so forth. God manifests his presence not as one who permits such suffering but as one whose will is set against it, as one who aligns himself on the side of humanity against all forms of inhumanity. It is here in such "contrast experiences" (the mysterious paradox of experiencing suffering that stands in contradiction to the experiencing of God's offered love) that God manifests himself as with us in the very moment of what is otherwise human failure. Schillebeeckx is able to illustrate this paradox with Christ's cry of dereliction from the cross: "My God, my God, why have you forsaken me?" (Mk 15:34), interpreting it not as an abandonment of Jesus by God but as Jesus' anguished cry of desolation at not being able to experience the succor of God in this moment of darkness even as he trusts entirely in the nearness of God that is in fact his continuing saving presence. This is made clear in subsequent verses of Psalm 22, which Jesus is citing, e.g., "He [God] has not hid his face from him, but has heard, when he cried out to him" (v. 24). Jesus thus entrusts to God what on the level of our history seems to be genuine failure but in reality is no such thing. The resurrection, then, is the manifestation of this abiding real presence of God to Jesus, which remained hidden, however, throughout his passion.

But what justifies this interpretation in which, rather than being absent, God is present and active in a hidden way in the face of human suffering? Only the fact that for the believer, the interpreted experience, through Scripture and tradition, of a revealing and saving God focuses on the meaning of the life, death, and resurrection of Jesus, which is first and foremost something negative; i.e., an opposition to everything that threatens or diminishes the truly human. Whereas some ambiguity remains, even in an appeal to the gospels as to what constitutes positively the fulfillment of the truly human, no such hesitancy is felt in opposition to everything that dehumanizes and threatens humanity. If it be true that, in the unquenchable search for meaning, what is truly worthy of humankind is not something already given beforehand but something for which we strive, the Christian believer trusts that whereas "everything is decided in our history . . . the last word is not with history, but with the God who lives with us" (*Christ*, p. 831).* God's overcoming of human failure is not subsequent to that failure but is being accomplished during and in the historical moment of failure itself—as was the case with Christ on his cross. Thus, our experience of redemption and salvation occurs only in passing and fragmentary ways as we entrust our failures to God in hoping for the future that looks to his promises. Christianity thus acknowledges that God comes to us as we really are—"he loved us while we were still in our sins" (Rom 5:8)—and saves us for life as much as from our sins. Schillebeeckx's theology does not flee from a world where negative experiences abound; rather, it forcefully asserts a calm confidence in God as a God for humanity and is marked by an unshakable joy in believing in this God "whose honor is the happiness of humankind."

A Christian orthopraxis, then, that "lives out" the doctrines is not at all individualistic; rather, with its new risks and ambiguities it occurs only within the context of a concrete Christian community. Schillebeeckx himself has declared, "I do not accept the possibility of having a Christianity or a Christian community that is not ecclesial." It is the ecclesial community that is the bearer of truth, and the role of theology becomes that of a hermeneutics of Christian practice. Theologians bring this praxis to theoretical and technical language that the community then tests against the norms of its own experience. The teaching office of the church is not then a mere deposit of truths, a bureau of orthodoxy, but a genuine pastoral office that seeks the doctrines entrusted to the church in the gospel, in tradition, and in the lives of Christians. The magisterium is not itself a theological locus but the final judge of the truths found in the theological loci. It alone passes judgment in an authoritative way because of its charism of being

---

*For the purpose of citations from Schillebeeckx's major Christological works *Jesus: An Experiment in Christology* and *Christ: The Experience of Jesus as Lord,* we will use the short titles *Jesus* and *Christ,* respectively.

able to call upon the Holy Spirit—"who will teach you all things and remind you of all I have said to you" (Jn 14:26)—but it does so in a responsible manner, acknowledging that the Spirit continues to mediate truth through Christian lives lived in a history of which the magisterium must take note. Its all-important role is one of negotiating that delicate balance of language that distinguishes truth from its distortions—as it did at Nicaea in the fourth century, at Chalcedon in the fifth, at Trent in the sixteenth, and at Vatican II in the twentieth century.

The specifically Christian contribution to this human solidarity against all forms of inhumanity lies in the acknowledgment that only God will give final meaning to history that will transform it into the kingdom. But it is *this* world that will be so transformed; eternity has already begun within the parameters of time. God's action in the world, moreover, is not in rivalry with that of humankind itself; human beings cannot expect to find God if they abandon the human condition. One of the richest of Schillebeeckx's concepts is that of "mediated immediacy," by which he means that while all contact with the divine is mediated through creatures, at the very heart of that mediation God mysteriously gives us nothing less than his uncreated self.

BACKGROUND: A THEOLOGIAN'S JOURNEY

The above synthesis represents in a nutshell the itinerary of one theologian's lifetime journey. The respective details and their implications will be worked out in a more generous and discursive manner in the nine chapters to come—all that has been presented here is an architectonic model of a complex whole. Its epicenter is surely the question concerning the historical mediation of the transcendent—one that successfully avoids the Scylla of deism on one hand the the Charybdis of pantheism on the other. As a hermeneutic of history and of Christian praxis, Schillebeeckx's theology views Christianity not as a privileged segment of universal history, namely, the chronicle of God's dealing with humanity through Israel and the Christ event, but of all of history seen from the vantage point of God himself as the Lord of history, as the one who ultimately gives meaning to history. The experience of our impotence in its negative way makes possible a positive experience, however fragmentary and provisional, of how

God seeks lovingly to transform the world—bearing in mind that it is this world, shaped by the initiatives of our freedom, that is being so transformed. If we do not directly register this transformation, it is because it transpires in a dimension proper to God himself; God, after all, in his immanence to creatures cannot cease to be God, cannot surrender his transcendence of all that is creaturely and finite. The most we are left with, then, is an analogous awareness of this transformation to which we can look in faith and hope. And since its consummation lies in the future, it is not something about which we know in theory but something for which we strive; it is more a matter of orthopraxis than of orthodoxy.

FAMILY AND REGIONAL BACKGROUND

What is now instructive and illuminating to ask is how Schillebeeckx has come to this theology in a new key. What a person is to become in the full maturity of life is determined by the myriad earlier influences that shape that becoming. But inversely, what a person ultimately makes of oneself sheds light on what was going on in the earlier formative processes. Edward Cornelis Florentius Alfons Schillebeeckx was born on November 12, 1914, in Antwerp, Belgium, the sixth of fourteen children of a middle-class Flemish family, and grew up in the nearby village of Kortenberg. His secondary education was in the hands of the Jesuits at Turnhout. In his familial ambiance Christianity was a pronounced formative factor, not at all a sanctimonious one, but a practical day-to-day personal appropriation of Catholic faith. Schillebeeckx recounts his father explaining that the child in the Christmas crèche was indeed God. He was a father who insisted on saying grace before meals in his own house even after the ordination of his son Edward. This perhaps explains to a degree Schillebeeckx's tendency to begin with the concrete and particular, deriving ideas and theories from life situations rather than vice versa. It is exemplified in the stress upon "orthopraxis" over "orthodoxy" that comes increasingly to the fore in his later theological writings. Dogmas are not only something that we confess in a cerebral way but something that we *do* and so determine behavior. This emphasis upon the practical also owes something to his Dutch background (he is Flemish-speaking), though the other side of the coin is his exposure to French *spiritualité*, the other cultural current in Belgium. At the risk of a vast oversimplification, the Flemish ingredient explains the social and political orientation in Schillebeeckx's Christian thought, while the French explains the leaning toward personal communing with God. His recent work has repeatedly emphasized two mediations of the transcendent to humankind: the political and ethical on one hand, the mystical and personally prayerful on the other.

THOMIST ORIGINS

Entering the Dominican order in 1934, whose demanding intellectualism tempered with a humanist spirit he found congenial, Schillebeeckx found himself confronted with the neo-Thomist revival inaugurated by Pope Leo XIII in the encyclical *Aeterni Patris* (1879) and implemented to a considerable extent by Jacques Maritain and Etienne Gilson. This program was intensified considerably by the condemnations of modernism by Pope Pius X in 1907 in the decree *Lamentabile* and the encyclical *Pascendi*. The neo-Thomist revival was an attempt to confront modernity, but from the very start it engaged modern thought in the interest of refuting it on the assumption that from Descartes onward modern thought had taken an erroneous turn. Schillebeeckx's own theological nurture, at the French Dominican faculty of theology at Saulchoir, just south of Paris, took place in the general ambiance of this revival but with significant distinguishing characteristics of its own deriving from the influence of Marie-Dominique Chenu and Yves Congar. Two lasting convictions from this experience were an understanding that God's self-disclosure is not a mere occurrence of the past but a continuing phenomenon mediated through contemporary cultural realities and an awareness that the recovery of the thought of Aquinas meant a reconstruction of the historical context in which it came to birth, which allowed that thought to reemerge in a way that challenged the rationalistic and conceptualist interpretation being put upon it by neo-Thomism. What has issued from this is a pronounced and perduring emphasis upon the primacy of God as Creator in the order of being and as Savior in the order of grace.

The former of these acknowledges that God is not homogeneous to anything that forms part of this world; God "lives" in a domain of intelligibility radically distinct from that of the thing-like entities of the cosmos. St. Thomas expressed this by naming God not as any sort of essence having existence (not even as the infinite and most perfect of beings), but as the sheer act of existing itself, which escapes objectification in any finite concept; God subsists as Be-ing, subsists in, grammatically speaking, the participial sense of the term. It is less proper to say he is in the world than that the world is in him, much as it is truer to speak of the body being in the soul than of the soul being in the body. He (so to speak) "empties out" himself to make room for a universe of creatures who possess, however, as their own the existence given them by God and sustained by him. The root explanation of the divine immanence to all reality is then precisely the divine transcendence; it is because God is the cause of the human creature's very act of freedom that such a creature can be free in the first place.

The primal sin, then, is the denial of our creatureliness. Even in freeing us from sin God does not enable us to escape the limitations necessarily inherent in our finitude. This explains that the first cause of our defects and failures lies with ourselves, with that weightiness of our being toward the nothingness from which it was called into existence. Evil arises from initiatives of our own that shatter, or at least neutralize, the divine initiatives toward being and goodness.

Implicit in this worldview is a quiet confidence in our ability to know God. However faintly, creaturely perfections mirror forth their creator, enabling us to know God in this indirect way—somewhat after the fashion in which a painting reflects the artist who painted it. It is not that God possesses these created qualities even to an infinite degree, but that they provide us with vectors *from which* we can name God in a vastly inadequate yet truthful way, one tailored to our humanity. The play of language, then, when it stretches out to the realm of the divine, engages a distinctive world of meaning, a second level of discourse. This rescues us from the silence of agnosticism in allowing us to speak of what remains shrouded in mystery, using concepts and images that *name* God but cannot *represent* him. We know him in a conscious unknowing, which means we are aware that we do not know him as he is in himself.

All of this, however, is a prerogative of humankind on the level of what belongs to it by nature, in the sphere of the relationship between creature and creator, leaving God in a certain anonymity that falls short of a deeply personal communion with him. Yet the latter is mysteriously desired and sought after (Aquinas speaks of a natural desire to see God) even as it remains impossible for us to implement—an ontological impossibility that is radicalized and ratified by our sinful alienation from God. But what is impossible to humankind in its natural constitution is made an actuality by grace, i.e., by God's gracious summoning of us to intersubjectivity with himself. Our freedom, our subjectivity, is made into an orientation and an openness toward the absolute subject who is God. Human freedom (which belongs to us as "made in the image of God"), while first of all a horizontal transcendence, is rooted in a vertical transcendence that is in turn transformed into a genuine trans-ascendance toward personal intersubjectivity with God in faith, hope, and love.

CONTRIBUTION FROM PHENOMENOLOGY

Schillebeeckx's rediscovery of the authentic thought of Aquinas, his fixing from within of the spirit of that "metaphysics of faith," is of course an interpretation of Thomas. It is an interpretation dominated by the illuminating insights achieved in the twentieth-century philosophical movement known as phenomenology, (among whose principal exponents were Edmund Husserl, Martin Heidegger, and Maurice Merleau-Ponty) to which Schillebeeckx was introduced by a fellow Dominican, Dominic De Petter, under whom he studied philosophy at the University of Louvain. Most influential here perhaps for the theology to come is the category of "encounter" as the fundamental mode of existing in the world proper to the existent that is human and personal. It is a structure of embodied consciousness focusing on the body as the point of insertion in the world; the body is not primarily an object among all the other things in the world but rather a subject that gives rise to a unique mode of contact between consciousness and the world. What is properly human, then, is an instance of incarnate subjectivity characterized by an awareness that precedes our objectives and impersonal knowledge of things. Encounter is thus the ground of interpersonal awareness and of that openness of existence that is in fact coexistence. Bodiliness is thus the locus for the emergence and expression of meaning; it is the sacrament of the self.

Obviously, this has rich implications for Christian, and especially for Catholic, theology. The incarnation as God's assumption of humanity, and so of our human bodiliness, makes Christ to be the primordial sacrament of our encounter with God. As a man among men and women, Jesus renders the hidden God and his saving intentions manifest in our very midst and draws believers into a personal and intersubjective closeness with God, who offers to us his very self. At the juncture of this bodiliness in its spatiality and temporality—both in its natural and eucharistic modes—there transpires the phenomenon of revelation as an intercommunion between God and humankind. Here phenomenological thought opens up an enriched understanding of the mystery of divine grace, especially in its modalities of revelation and faith. The traditional Thomistic axiom that "grace presupposes nature" is newly illumined by this. Supernatural grace is not simply something superimposed upon nature from without, endowing nature with capabilities beyond anything of which it is capable by itself. Rather, the human being already stands before the face of God as a personal absolute in purely natural existence; this is a depth dimension to the concrete historical condition of being situated in the world with other men and women. The concrete experience of existence is such that the objective and ontic dynamism of experienced reality carries the human—in a way as yet only implicit, prereflexive, and unthematized—to God as the personal ground of all reality in what becomes an act of implicit intuition. This natural reference to and awareness of God belongs to the very being of humanity and is an intrinsic condition for the very possibility of revelation. But it undergoes a transformation with God's loving and gratuitous offer of communion with himself, which is either freely assented to or freely rejected. Thus there is now no purely natural human life, because of God's universal saving will. God now gives himself directly to those disposed to believe. This is done not only through created realities of the world—even though awareness of this divine self-communication cannot be otherwise than in terms of those realities and the concepts, images, and narratives expressive of them. God as he is in his inmost self renders himself present to us in what may be called paradoxically a "mediated immediacy."

An important conclusion flows from this reconception of the nature/grace—or more accurately, the reason/faith—problematic. If Christian faith terminates at the reality revealed (ultimately God himself) though necessarily in an unthematic way that can only be thematized inadequately in finite concepts and symbols directly expressive of created realities, then such thematizations, including those that acquire the status of dogma, necessarily and spontaneously are subject to a process of continuous reinterpretation. In short, all of this offers grounds for a theory of development of dogma.

FROM DOGMA TO CRITICAL HERMENEUTICS

An important consequence of employing phenomenology as an interpetative key in theological reflection is the abandonment of a dogmatic starting point in theology. Rather than starting with truths taken on faith as revealed by God and seeking to unfold their meaning, the theologian begins with an analysis of the subject to whom such revelation is made, i.e., with reflection upon the mystery of human existence in the world. This gives a central role to hermeneutics, the science of interpretation that seeks to recover the meaning of the past for the present in a confrontation of Christianity with modernity. Here, the thought of Martin Heidegger became a dominant influence that was imported into Christian theology by Rudolf Bultmann: all understanding is self-understanding. The gospels then are not meant to convey otherwise unavailable information about God and his intentions vis-à-vis humankind but to articulate the self-understanding of the first disciples made possible by their contact with Jesus of Nazareth. Theology as hermeneutics will then strive to reproduce that encounter with God through the life and death of Jesus in such wise that God's revelatory word will be translated into contemporary culture and its meaning for us released. The difficulty with this early phase of hermeneutics was that too much rode on the subjectivity of the believer, on a "decisionism" that is an interpretation of the *kerygma* rather than of the Christ event, which lies behind it and is its ground. The Word of God is invested with an authority that is not established historically; indeed there is an escape from history into the safe harbor of the decision of faith.

The corrective to this way of thinking was supplied by Wolfhart Pannenberg in insisting that encounter with God does not occur other than historically, making it necessary to get behind the *kerygma* to the events that are its origin. Interpretation is not separate from the facts and superimposed upon them by the interpreter (a Kantian principle) but resident in the facts themselves as understood in the movement of history (Hegel's alternative to Kant). Now it is understood not only that revelation is historical (Bultmann) but that history universally taken (which universality comes only from history in its consummation anticipated in the resurrection of Jesus) constitutes revelation (Pannenberg). The meaning and meaningfulness for us of the past events recounted in the New Testament does not reside in a structural commonality of consciousness (ours and the first disciples) that allows that the Scriptures are directly inspired by God, but in the objective content of the events themselves when they are grasped in the context of a tradition that views the Scriptures as only witnessing to such meaning. Theology now is no longer a hermeneutics of the word of God but a hermeneutics of history.

So now the task of hermeneutics becomes not one of merely reinterpreting the past so that it might spring forth with fresh meaning for the present, but one of dialectically relating theory and praxis so that the latter can be both the proving ground for the former and the matrix of a genuinely new and enriched understanding of theoretical truth. Orthodoxy and orthopraxis thus remain inseparable, but a certain primacy is given to the latter as transforming Christian existence and thus opening the way to a new future.

But this awareness of the hermeneutical task of theology leads to another realization. If theology is charged with the task of reinterpreting and transforming the past (without doing violence to it), then it has to be aware that the past is mediated with the constant risk of some distortion. Theology then cannot neglect its *critical* function, both of discerning such aberrations and of disclaiming any absolute claim for present utopian projects. Followers of Christ cannot fail to strive after all that makes for human healing and renewal, with the political struggle for peace and justice in the world. But by the same token we must be aware that none of the changes we succeed in making will themselves bring about the kingdom of God. Christianity cannot lay claim to knowing positively what is ultimately worthy of humankind and constitutive of its destiny, apart from the resurrection of Christ, which is in the mode of a promise to which believers look with hope. But it can know what threatens the truly human and thus align itself against all forms of evil and suffering. The positive contribution of Christianity toward the full humanization of humankind is the realization that critical rationality and humanism, however loftily conceived, are not enough. We strive for the truly human only in union with God who has made "the cause of humankind to be his [God's] cause." In the end it is God who will establish the kingdom. Yet it remains true that our eschatological hope is not a flight from this world and its history, for they remain the stage whereupon the gradual fulfillment takes shape. Our striving under God is then the anticipation of the kingdom to come; for now, we are a people in exodus.

Thus Schillebeeckx can write "everything has been given to us and everything has yet to be done" (*Christ,* p. 514). Everything depends then on God's free gift of grace, and yet grace is real only as implemented by human freedom in the response of faith. But God is already enlisted on the side of humankind against all that dehumanizes. This means that even in human failure and the suffering that comes in its wake, God remains at the side of men and women. It is not that God is absent now from human disaster but will be present and active in the eschatological future to then set things right. Rather, God is present precisely in failure. Christian faith is steadfastness in this conviction, in "this awareness of being grounded in God, of persisting when every empirical foundation and every guarantee have been removed and one weeps over the fiasco of one's life" (*Christ,* p. 815). To the extent that one can be aware of this nearness of God, it can be experienced not in the mode of positive support but only in the mode of absence, because this incomprehensible immediacy is the immediacy of God, which paradoxically is real only in its finite mediations. As soon as it is sought directly in itself, it vanishes, eluding finite attempts to grasp it. If this be so, it follows that "*ultimate* failure, *definitive* evil and *unreconciled* suffering have their real, final and terrifying form only in human reluctance and inability to love" (*Christ*, p. 831). What Christian faith confesses in all of this is "the continuity between the hidden dimension of what took place on the cross and its manifestation in the resurrection of Jesus, though we are not in a position to make a theoretical reconciliation of the human experience of failure and the religious experience of the redemptive triumph of God *in* this failure" (*Christ*, p. 831).

Not to be overlooked amidst these academic achievements is a strong pastoral concern, a personal commitment intense and even passionate in kind, blending together theory and practice, that has expressed itself recently in his addressing the issue of nuclear disarmament. Schillebeeckx was summoned to Rome to defend certain of his theological positions before church authorities. He did so in irenic fashion, without rancor, witnessing personally to his conviction that the mystery of salvation in Jesus is always mediated to us by the living tradition of the community of believers that is the church. Yet this was done without compromising the sense of how indispensable to the church is the role of the critical scholar who must not only reverence the past but interpret it as well. In all of this, we catch a glimpse of the deep simplicity and unpretentiousness that mark his own faith that "only truth can be the soul of a free community of men and women," especially that community that lives by faith in "the God who has made the cause of humankind to be his [God's] own cause." Schillebeeckx's own life, even more than his work, has emphasized graphically that we wait for the future by shaping it now and that believers live out in the present the promises of God like a leaven that quickens and renews.

Thus, at the heart of the theology of Edward Schillebeeckx as it develops organically through a variety of methodologies, drawing richly but critically from all of them, there lies a manifest thematic unity—albeit one that lives and so grows. It is that of the absolute primacy of God and his grace, construed at first metaphysically, wherein God is the pure act of "to be," then anthropologically, i.e., with reference to humankind and its free future, wherein God is the redeemer of history, and finally in a strictly theological way, wherein God's primacy is that of uncreated and altruistic love— this God who is revealed in Jesus the Christ as a God whose honor is the happiness of men and women.

This primal theme is displayed by Schillebeeckx in countless books and articles on sacraments, faith, revelation, Christ, redemption, eschatology, Mary, the church, hermeneutics, the Eucharist, marriage, ministry, laity, and liberation theology. The chapters that follow single out these central concerns in an attempt to implement and clarify this suggestive theology in enriching detail.

SUGGESTIONS FOR FURTHER READING

For further background on Schillebeeckx and his thought see Ted Schoof, "Masters in Israel: VII," *Clergy Review* 55 (1970): 943–60; John Bowden, *Edward Schillebeeckx: In Search of the Kingdom of God* (New York: Crossroad, 1983); and Schillebeeckx's own *God Is New Each Moment.* For a sampling of the wide range of theological topics addressed and a complete bibliography (401 entries in all) of Schillebeeckx's writings from 1945 to 1983, see Robert Schreiter, ed., *The Schillebeeckx Reader.* A documented summary of Schillebeeckx's controversy with the Congregation for the Doctrine of the Faith can be found in Ted Schoof, ed., *The Schillebeeckx Case.* A popularized version of many salvational themes central to Schillebeeckx's theology is available in a collection of his homilies entitled *God Among Us: The Gospel Proclaimed.*

2. Interpretation and Method

WILLIAM L. PORTIER

THE QUESTION OF METHOD IN
CONTEMPORARY CATHOLIC THOUGHT

The appearance of a chapter on method near the beginning of this thematic introduction to Schillebeeckx's thought makes a statement about the discipline of theology in the contemporary Western academy. Among academic theologians, especially in the United States, the topic of "method in theology"—the question about what theology is and how to do it—is vigorously debated. The term "theological method" refers to the approach one takes to the task of theology. To discuss theological method is to give an account of the terms one uses in conceiving that task and to show what is required, e.g., in the way of ancillary disciplines, to carry out the task of theology. The purpose of this chapter, then, is to explain the distinguishing features of Schillebeeckx's approach to the theological task. First, however, it is necessary to explain why method is an issue in contemporary Catholic thought.

Ever since the advent of the "new science" and its overthrow of the traditional worldview at the beginning of the modern period, Western thought has preoccupied itself with the question of method. René Descartes's *Discourse on Method* (1637) voices this concern in its classic form. As the church struggled with its response to modernity, modern thinkers not only questioned the value of monarchy in political life but also the validity of appeals to authority as a way to truth in intellectual and religious matters. A major development occurred in 1879 when, with his encyclical *Aeterni Patris*, Pope Leo XIII launched a massive revival of scholastic method in philosophy and theology.

Unlike medieval scholasticism, which was an organic part of an emerging civilization, the neoscholasticism of the Thomistic revival was self-consciously antimodern. Scholastic method emphasized logical relationships and metaphysical distinctions among the various truths witnessed to by the disparate array of biblical and patristic sources. Since the historical contexts of truth claims were considered logically and metaphysically irrelevant, historical concerns were systematically absent from scholastic thought. This rendered Leo XIII's renewed scholasticism singularly ill-equipped to deal with the nineteenth century's emerging sense of the methodological importance of considerations of time and place, i.e., of history. With some notable exceptions, neoscholastic method tended to dominate Catholic intellectual life from the time of Leo XIII until the "return to the sources" (*ressourcement*) that preceded and prepared the way for the Second Vatican Council in 1962.

After the council, many Catholic thinkers abandoned scholastic methodology, finding it inadequate to the needs of contemporary life and thought. With the collapse of the public language and common set of assumptions provided by scholastic method, the modern methodological problematic raised many troubling questions for ill-prepared Catholic thinkers: How should theology's proper field of inquiry be located and marked off? What should count as relevant evidence in theological argumentation? Should philosophy be the only mediating device for communicating the truth of Christianity to Westerners, or does it need to be supplemented by other disciplines such as history and the social sciences? These questions by their nature underscore the range of possible theological methods and the necessity of identifying each theologian's particular approach.

During the period of renewal in theology that preceded Vatican II, two Jesuit thinkers who lived from 1904 to 1984 stand out as particularly creative and influential in their attempts to engage neoscholasticism in a dialogue with modern thought: Karl Rahner and Bernard Lonergan. With greater or less appropriateness, and partly under the influence of Otto Muck's *The Transcendental Method* (1968), their thought has been lumped together and designated as "transcendental method" or "transcendental Thomism." In a very general way, transcendental method deals with the process of reasoning to the necessary conditions of the possibility, in the human subject, of whatever philosophical or the-

ological issue is under discussion. The issue might be the phenomenon of human knowing or the belief that humans have heard a
revelation from God or that God has become human in Jesus
Christ. Rahner's early thought is preoccupied with questions
about what kind of beings humans have to be for these beliefs to
be true.

The voices of Rahner and Lonergan have shaped the discussion of theological method that emerged after the Vatican council. Lonergan's magisterial *Method in Theology* (1972) addresses
the issue explicitly. The theological education of significant
numbers among the present generation of professors in Catholic
seminaries and graduate schools of theology included a powerful
dose of transcendental method. Consequently, the thought of
Rahner and Lonergan, especially that of the former, holds a certain position of dominance in the Catholic theological academy
in North America.

As a theology professor in the divinity school at the University
of Chicago, David Tracy has developed Lonergan's thought in an
attempt to ensure the academic legitimacy of theology within the
American political framework of separation of church and state.
In this context, the foundational question about whether confes-
sional religious faith is a necessary dimension in theological inquiry becomes central. In his *Analogical Imagination* (1981), Tracy
sketched what he called a "social portrait of the theologian." He
argued that the answer to the question "what is theology?" depends in significant measure on the answer to the prior question
"to whom do theologians think they are talking?" Tracy identified three possible reference groups or "publics" for theological
discourse: society, academy, and church.

In these terms, we could say, at the risk of oversimplification,
that Rahner's primary public is the church, especially those
groups such as clergy and religious who have a deep interest in
the maintenance and renewal of the church's present forms. Lonergan's focus is more directly on the academic sector of the
church public, asking how theology can maintain itself as a discipline under modern conditions. Tracy carries this discussion into
the academy at large.

In the context of contemporary Catholic theology, Schillebeeckx occupies a distinctive position in relation to the ap-

proaches of the other major theologians mentioned here. In this chapter, the question of his method, his understanding of what theologians do, will be addressed, as Tracy suggests, by first inquiring about the audience Schillebeeckx thinks he is addressing.

SCHILLEBEECKX'S PUBLIC AND THE DUTCH CATHOLIC EXPERIENCE

The Dutch Catholic experience during and after Vatican II has shaped Schillebeeckx's understanding of the public to whom his theology is addressed. Like Rahner, Lonergan, and Tracy, Schillebeeckx has spent most of his life as a theology professor, a member of a professional elite in both church and society. Strangely enough, however, he doesn't consider his primary public to be the academy. Nor is his intended public narrowly ecclesiastical.

In the one-page foreword to his *Jesus* book, Schillebeeckx makes an astounding statement about his intended audience. On the opening page of this more than seven-hundred-page digest of, and theological reflection upon, the entire range of twentieth-century scholarship on Jesus in the synoptic Gospels, the author dares to claim that the work is not addressed to the questions "that normally preoccupy academics," but rather to the questions "that seem most urgent to the ordinary Christian." The "ordinary Christians" among us can judge for themselves whether he has been successful. In any case this brief text reveals one of the most significant and distinguishing features of Schillebeeckx's thought—his intended public. He insists that in the *Jesus* book he has "tried to bridge the gap between academic theology and the concrete needs of the ordinary Christian." He claims that, although this task calls for a "certain amount of academically disciplined work," he has written the *Jesus* book with a minimum of theological jargon and "in such a way as one might suppose would put the contents within reach of anybody interested."

Although Schillebeeckx brings considerable academic resources to bear on his work, he rarely addresses the methodological question that so exercises contemporary theology. He hardly ever uses the term "method" and probably regards the methodological problematic sketched above as abstract and rationalistic. He might insist, as he does in the preface to *Interim Report on the Books "Jesus" and "Christ"* that, "Methodology only becomes possible when one begins to reflect on the actual method of interpretation used in a particular study." Perhaps because of his long tenure in the state-supported Catholic faculty of theology at Nijmegen, he has not had to face the question of theology's legitimacy in the academy in precisely the terms posed by David Tracy. He is therefore quite comfortable describing himself in traditional terms as a believer who reflects. His methodological interludes often contain variations on the Anselmian *fides quaerens intellectum* (faith seeking understanding). He feels no need to offer a reasoned defense of faith's constitutive role in theology.

His public is therefore more the church than the academy. But it is the church conceived in a particular way, as a community of participating believers who are also part of society or the world—albeit a prophetic part—rather than ranged against society and the world in resignation and resentment. The church is not conceived in terms of "the elitist experiences of intellectual clerics," (*Interim Report*, p. 4), but as made up of believers who are also active participants in Dutch, West German, or North American culture and society.

The experience of Dutch Catholicism has decisively shaped Schillebeeckx's understanding of the church to which his theological reflections are addressed. As theologian extraordinaire, first to the bishops, especially Cardinal Bernard Alfrink of Utrecht to whom the *Jesus* book is dedicated, and the Dutch Pastoral Council, and then later to the so-called critical communities of Dutch Christians upon whose experiences his theology of ministry claims to be a reflection, he has served as a kind of theological midwife for a new way of experiencing the church in the Netherlands. This experience in turn has had a profound impact on his conception of theology. Although the situation of the church in Holland differs significantly from our experience of it in North America, there are enough similarities to account for the veritable invasion of North American Catholicism by Dutch authors in translation after the Vatican council.

Schillebeeckx's theology is thoroughly "contextual" and its context is the Dutch Catholic experience since Vatican II. According to an arrangement known as "columnization," the Dutch

Reformed, Roman Catholics, and socialists each form one of the pillars or columns holding up the common arch of Dutch society. This is, in a sense, a thoroughly modern arrangement with each interest group guaranteed access to the public forum in keeping with the modern values of democratic pluralism. At the same time, the traditional identity of each column is preserved by means of state support for its separate institutions such as schools, hospitals, and media of mass communication. Pressure to introduce the democratic, pluralistic values of the public sphere into the Catholic column began to build up during the 1950s. This pressure to "break through" columnization coincided with the Second Vatican Council and produced the unique experience of Dutch Catholicism during the 1960s.

The parallels with the Catholic experience in the United States during the same period are striking. The immigrant church had produced a separate or "ghetto" Catholicism with its own network of institutions. After the World War II, as later-generation immigrants assimilated the values and life-styles of the wider culture, pressure built up to introduce some of these values into the church itself. The Second Vatican Council's reforms coincided with a period of singular turbulence in society at large. A key difference between the U.S. and Dutch experiences of renewal after Vatican II is that, by means of state support, separate Catholic institutions in Holland were able to maintain themselves with relative ease in spite of decolumnization. With their institutional maintenance guaranteed, Catholics like Schillebeeckx can afford to be somewhat more open to contemporary trends. The similarity between the two experiences helps to account for the continuing popularity of Schillebeeckx's books in the United States. The significant difference could give rise to the impression among U.S. readers that Schillebeeckx's openness to secular values is self-indulgent if not naive capitulation to current social and intellectual trends.

As the leading theologian in the Dutch Catholic church during the time of decolumnization, Schillebeeckx found himself cast in a quasi-public role as mediator or interpreter whose task was to justify present experiments in church life on the basis of appeals to the historical tradition. This role helps to account for Schillebeeckx's sense that his own public extends beyond the academy and lends plausibility to his claim that he writes for the ordinary believer.

Lonergan has defined theology as the mediation between a religion and a culture. In the Dutch church before, during, and after the Vatican council, Schillebeeckx has served such a bridging function. In the early days of renewal, he interpreted the Catholic tradition to the Dutch church, helping to shape the new experience of the church in the Netherlands. He then found himself in the position of having to reflect theologically on these new experiences in the light of the tradition. He has mediated between the universal church with its diverse tradition and the Dutch church as one of its contemporary localizations. More recently, as in his two books on ministry during the 1980s, he has mediated between extreme elements in the Dutch church and the Roman authorities.

THEOLOGY AS INTERPRETATION: FROM HISTORY TO HERMENEUTICS TO CRITICAL THEORY

OVERVIEW

Because his public is not limited to academic theologians but extends to ordinary believers as members of a secular society, Schillebeeckx's approach to theology has come more and more to center on the interpretation of experience, both past Christian experience and the experience of contemporary believers. He wants to assist in the creation of new forms and possibilities for Christian experience. His understanding of what theologians do is rooted in his own experience. A key term that he has used consistently over the past twenty years to describe the theological task is *interpretation.* As his thought develops, this term takes on an ever more concrete meaning. Far from being a personal, theoretical activity, theology as interpretation entails concrete social dimensions with inseparable links to Christian life and worship. This means that Christians don't simply have experience and then abstractly interpret it in Christian terms. Rather Christians are people who actually *experience* life—and don't *merely* interpret it—in terms of the story of Jesus Christ. In keeping with this concrete sense of interpretation, he has more recently come to refer to theology as the mutually critical correlation between Christian sources and contemporary Christian experience and the critical reflection on Christian praxis.

To the "ordinary believer" these various descriptions of theology might sound like theological jargon. But each phrase finds its home and a rather precise referent in the sets of questions involved in one or more of the various auxiliary conceptual frameworks that Schillebeeckx uses in his theological reflection. While a familiarity with transcendental method might enable one to predict with some accuracy what Rahner or Lonergan might say about a particular theological question, Schillebeeckx's positions are more volatile and unpredictable. He is rather like a master chef who doesn't cook from recipes but simply has a sense for the right ingredient. To speak of "method" in Schillebeeckx's theology, then, is not to speak in the usual terms of the discussion of theological method in the academy. Although he is a Dominican and trained in the thought of St. Thomas Aquinas, he is neither a neoscholastic nor a transcendental Thomist. His is not the "transcendental method" of Rahner and Lonergan, nor does he have a theological system that could be expressed in a dogmatics such as the great twentieth-century Protestant theologians Karl Barth and Paul Tillich have produced. Most of his writings are occasional, i.e., addressed to specific concerns that have arisen in the church and society in which he participates.

As Schillebeeckx himself might put it, human experience, and hence revelation as well, have a narrative structure. A helpful way to clarify his various descriptions of the theological task, e.g., interpretation, mutually critical correlation, or critical reflection on Christian praxis, might be to place them in the setting of the story of his career as a theologian in and to the Dutch church. A brief summary of his movement from history in the form of a presentation of the results of *ressourcement* in the interpersonal categories of phenomenology (1957–1966) to hermeneutics (1966–1971) to critical theory (1971 to the present) will precede a more detailed account of how Schillebeeckx's understanding of the nature of theology has developed from the end of the Vatican Council to the present in dialogue with hermeneutic philosophy and the Frankfurt School's critical theory of society. Each of these intellectual developments finds its concrete context in the Dutch Catholic experience. Pivotal dates are 1966 and 1971: 1966

marks the beginning of the Dutch Pastoral Council and efforts to
bring modern values into the life of the church; 1971 marks the
beginnings of polarization within the Dutch church, the rise of
the critical communities, and the attempt to achieve some critical
distance from modernity.

The path Schillebeeckx's thought has followed since Vatican II
is representative of the personal and intellectual development of
many other Catholic theologians. From the Thomism of his early
training, he moved to the kind of existential phenomenology popular in post–World War II France where he studied. In his *Christ
the Sacrament of the Encounter with God* he used the interpersonal
categories of phenomenology to make the results of his historical
research on the sacraments available to a contemporary audience.
Once within the orbit of the phenomenological movement, Schillebeeckx discovered hermeneutics and its promise for better understanding of the dogmatic tradition of Christianity.

Hermeneutics, the art of understanding or interpreting another's meaning, with proper qualifications, can be used synony-
mously with the term *interpretation*. In hermeneutic philosophy,
the interpretation or understanding of a text in its context becomes a metaphor for the human phenomenon of understanding
or interpretation in general.

Criticisms of hermeneutics as too theoretical by Jürgen Habermas (b. 1929) and other neo-Marxist social theorists led Schillebeeckx to "critical theory" with its focus on the unavoidable
political or praxis dimension of all interpretation and experience.
Critical theory attempts to exploit one of the fundamental insights of the Marxist tradition—now a commonplace in a variety
of forms of social thought—that the interpretation of any tradition likely involves systematic distortions of communication in
the interests of those who have power and privilege. This discovery that communication or interpretation within a given tradition
can be systematically skewed lies at the root of all present forms of
"critical" or "contextual" theology, from feminist theology in the
industrial West to liberation theology in Latin America. Within
the framework of critical theory, therefore, faithful interpretation becomes, in significant measure, a function of ethical and political commitment to act in a way that will minimize such

distortion. As the Gospel of John points out, the truth is something we must do rather than simply know.

Throughout all of these developments, Schillebeeckx's abiding concern has been to make the experience of Christ more real for contemporary believers. This overriding interest permeates his thought from his early work on the sacraments to the massive and still unfinished christological trilogy begun in the 1970s. The question about the experience of the reality of God, the presence of the absolute in finite forms in human language and history, has preoccupied him in various conceptual forms from his earlier interest in the development of doctrine to his present concern with what might be termed the continuity of Christian experience.

1966–1971: HERMENEUTICS AND THE DIALOGUE WITH MODERNITY

But for the intervention of the Second Vatican Council, Schillebeeckx may have spent his life in relative academic obscurity at the University of Nijmegen. Instead he became a theological consultant to the Dutch bishops, a significant if unofficial presence at the council and, most importantly, a key architect of the experiment of Dutch Catholicism during the period of decolumnization and the council. During this time, Dutch Catholicism gave birth to a new sense of being the church, characterized by "grass roots" lay participation and "collegiality" and understood as the maximum lay involvement consistent with Catholic ecclesiology. It began with a nationwide network of discussion groups early in the decade and culminated in the Dutch Pastoral Council, which opened in 1966 and held its fully representative sessions between 1968 and 1970. The publicly supported resources of the Catholic column were put at the service of introducing the political freedoms of modern Western society into church life insofar as this was judged to be theologically possible.

As did U.S. Catholicism during the same period, the Dutch Catholic experience of the 1960s doubtless produced excess and abuse. But it also generated an intense spirit of optimism and enthusiasm. Using the terminology of Emile Durkheim, sociologist John A. Coleman has described it as an experience of "collective effervescence." This spirit has left its permanent mark on Schillebeeckx's theological style. Apart from it, one would be hard put to account of the urgent tone, the hopeful spirit, and even the occasional nature of Schillebeeckx's theology. Likewise it is difficult to avoid the conclusion that his theology has become the primary bearer or mediator of what Coleman calls "a new set of collective symbols for the church" (*Evolution,* p. 164). Words such as "grass roots," "collegiality," "dialogue," and "the future" are among these symbols. Schillebeeckx's historical sense helped to set this experience in motion; subsequently he would try to give it shape and direction. Until the polarization that occurred after the 1971 synod at Rome, in part over the issue of clerical celibacy, he performed this mediating function for the Dutch church at large. During the next decade, the experiences of those Christians he described in the *Ministry* book and in *God Is New Each Moment* as "critical communities" became the object of his theological reflection.

In the process of assisting at the birth of new forms of Dutch Catholicism during the 1960s, Schillebeeckx began to experience his role as a theologian in a new way. The previous generation's emphasis on historical recovery of the sources of Christian doctrine and worship as a way of clarifying their present meaning gave way to deeper questions about the role of the present and the future in the faithful interpretation of the past. With the contemporary setting changing so rapidly itself, its role in shaping our interpretations of the historical context of the tradition became more clear. Contemporary Christian experience would have to be located within a fusion of these two settings or horizons, with the contemporary setting the only available medium for interpreting the past. Such considerations led Schillebeeckx from what might be termed "historical sense" to what David Tracy calls "historical consciousness" and Bernard Lonergan calls "historical mindedness." Thus by the mid-1960s Schillebeeckx had entered the universe of discourse of hermeneutic philosophy.

This discovery of the historical interpreter's own historicity proved too heady for many during this period. But the move to historical consciousness need not end in an absolute and hopeless sense of historical relativity. First, absolute historical relativism self-destructs in inner contradition as soon as one proclaims that all truths are relative. As Lonergan has explained, truths are not absolutely or simply relative but relative to a time and place. Times and places are connected and the study of these connections is called history. The human act of interpretation or understanding is therefore profoundly historical. As Schillebeeckx would learn from critical theory during the next decade, the study of history or the intepretation of tradition opens out onto ethics and politics. Absolute historical relativism is nothing more than a form of ethical paralysis whose only practical effect is to maintain the status quo.

At the very time when Dutch Catholics were trying to integrate the modern secular values of freedom and pluralism into church structures on a grand scale, certain theologians in the United States were elaborating a form of theology that in hindsight appears incredibly naive and one-dimensional in its affirmation of modern Western culture. During an extended tour of the United States late in the decade, Schillebeeckx encountered the theology of secularization and the death of God and found aspects of it congenial for interpreting the recent experience of Dutch Catholicism. This encounter set the stage for a serious consideration of the question of Christianity and culture in the early 1970s and for the reconceiving of theology as the mutually critical correlation of Christian tradition and contemporary experience. At this point, however, contemporary experience in the form of the theology of secularization threatened to overwhelm the Christian tradition.

A group of young theological colleagues, students of J. B. Metz at Münster, challenged Schillebeeckx's brief flirtation with the theology of secularization and the overidentification with modern Western culture it implied. These "theologians of contestation," as he called them, his fellow Dominican Karl Derksen and the Belgian Marcel Xhaufflaire among others, forced Schillebeeckx to deal more seriously with "critical theory." Schillebeeckx was already familiar with Habermas, the chief proponent of critical theory, from Habermas's debate with Hans Georg Gadamer. But the challenge of these young theologians certainly accelerated his examination of this new movement.

Denouncing the theology of secularization as an unquestioning capitulation to modernity, Xhaufflaire drew upon the resources of critical theory to call for a "critical theology" that would no longer be content to accept modern secularism wholeheartedly without protest. He argued that theologians ought to reassess their assumptions about the relationship between theory and practice. In response Schillebeeckx reappraised as excessively theoretical the notion of interpretation he had learned from Martin Heidegger and the hermeneutic philosophers: "Our relationship with the past is never purely theoretical or hermeneutical" (*Christ*, p. 72). From this dialogue with critical theory has grown his present understanding of theology. Orthopraxis (right living) must be "an essential element of the hermeneutic process." In this conceptual framework, theology becomes reflective "self-consciousness of Christian praxis" or "the critical theory (in a specifically theological manner) of the praxis of faith" (*Understanding of Faith*, pp. 132, 143–44). The unfamiliar term "praxis" is used deliberately to avoid the connotations of the term "practice." "Practice" implies a prior pure theory that we then apply practically; "praxis" by contrast is understood as coconstitutive of theory likewise conceived. The ethical moment is therefore inseparable from theory or reflection. This is a contemporary rendering or recovery of the biblical and patristic truism that Christian thinking arises from and must return to Christian living.

1971–PRESENT: CRITICAL THEORY AND THE CRITIQUE OF MODERNITY

Critical theory arose in Germany during the Weimar years. It concerned itself with what Schillebeeckx might now call the "negative contrast experience" of a group of German Jewish intellectuals outraged by the ethical paralysis that afflicted traditional forms of theory in the German universities in the face of the obvious inhumanities of national socialism. These victims of Nazi barbarism voiced their criticism of modern Western rationality in two key notions, both of which had considerable impact on Schillebeeckx's thought: the dialectic of enlightenment and critical negativity of the negative dialectic. In May of 1986, Schillebeeckx began his Abraham Kuyper Lecture at the Free University of Amsterdam by noting the historical irony that the cultural forces of science and technology, widely hailed since the seventeenth century as liberating humans from bondage to nature, have succeeded instead in compounding human hunger and war and threatening the ultimate violence of nuclear destruction (*On Christian Faith*, p. 1). Since the history of reason began, with the Greeks, it has promised liberation from natural and religious forces only to deliver us into the bondage of humanly created forces. To this paradox of history, Max Horkheimer and Theodor Adorno, the progenitors of contemporary critical theory, gave the name "dialectic of enlightenment." As their colleague Herbert Marcuse might have put it, reason has become irrational.

The dialectic of enlightenment means that any theoretician from any discipline, including theology, who dares to give an account of the necessary rationality and meaning of the present order makes a mockery of all those voiceless ones on the margins, all those who have suffered and died needlessly for what passes in traditional theory for the rationality of the present order. To those who look at it from the underside, to those who suffer and have suffered at its hands, the present order can never be completely rational. Needless human suffering, the history of the "barbarous excess" of human suffering, as Schillebeeckx names it in the *Christ* book, cries out against any premature attempt to close the account of the present order's rationality. In the name of those who have suffered needlessly, irrationally, critical theory must protest against any attempt to force an ultimate human solution or interpretation on the human condition. This is the critical negativity of the negative dialectic, the need to deny ultimate political and social solutions to the human predicament as falling short of all inclusive freedom and rationality. As Horkheimer put it, "The whole is the lie."

In critical theory's concern for suffering humanity, Schillebeeckx finds resonances with Jesus' way of life. For the sake of the kingdom of God preached by Jesus, whose eschatological promise relativizes all human attempts at peace and order, Schillebeeckx embraces the negative dialectic as a fitting contribution to theology. But he finds fault with what he judges to be its inability to provide a positive vision that can serve as the basis for what he calls "political love" in the present. He looks for this needed vision in the story of Jesus Christ, in whose death and resurrection the kingdom of God and the history of true human freedom have already begun. In his monumental christological trilogy, begun in the 1970s after his encounter with critical theory, Schillebeeckx presents to contemporary readers, in the form of a narrative of Jesus' life based on the best New Testament scholarship he can find, his vision of the specific contribution that Christians can make to the needed salvation of a suffering world. In the Congregation for the Doctrine of the Faith's April 5, 1986, "Instruction on Christian Freedom and Liberation," Cardinal Joseph Ratzinger bears eloquent testimony to the religious relevance of such contributions in his concept of the "integral salvation of the world."

Schillebeeckx's christology has made critical theory's sensitivity to needless human suffering its own. In *Jesus* and *Christ* he has placed Jesus and his ignominious death on the cross among the numberless, voiceless victims in the long history of human suffering. God's saving presence and love need to be shown today as they were shown in Jesus' life and death and resurrection. Just as those who experienced Jesus experienced salvation from God, so Schillebeeckx thinks that today we can experience God's salvation in a particular way, in "negative contrast experiences" that reveal our need for God's salvation and in various short-of-ultimate liberations that reveal God's saving presence.

During the 1980s Schillebeeckx has often used the terms "mysticism" and "politics" to refer to such experiences. In public lectures geared to general audiences he has used these same terms to explain what theologians do. Although the experience of God mediated through mysticism and politics will be treated at greater length in Chapter 6, the categories merit brief mention here because Schillebeeckx has recently used them to explain what theology is. In 1982 the Dutch government awarded him, the first theologian so honored, the Erasmus prize for his contribution to European culture. Singled out for special notice was his critical posture toward the currently ambiguous and noninclusive functioning of Western values in the world. His remarks on this occasion, September 17, 1982, dwelt upon the theologian's responsibility in this situation. Noting theology's past complicity, he wrote: "But whatever one thinks of contemporary theologians, one thing should be granted them: by means of a historical praxis of commitment to mysticism and politics, they are trying to discover the human face of God and, starting from there, to revive hope in a society, a humanity with a more human face." He went on to describe the main task of theology: "to preserve the transcendence of the God who loves humankind, hidden and yet so near, in the face of the idols which human beings set up" (*God Among Us*, p. 253).

In *On Christian Faith: The Spiritual, Ethical and Political Dimensions*, the translation of his 1985 Abraham Kuyper Lectures, he treats mysticism and politics at length as historical developments of the two great commandments, love of God and love of neighbor. Mysticism and politics are the forms such love is likely to take among middle-class Christians, members of the relatively privileged classes in the dominant culture, citizens of nation-states that possess and threaten to use nuclear weapons. As one who reflects critically on Christian praxis, the theologian is sent to search this experience for the call and salvation of God. "Without prayer or mysticism," he concludes, "politics soon becomes cruel and barbaric; without political love, prayer or mysticism soon becomes sentimental uncommitted interiority" (p. 75).

CONCLUSION

Schillebeeckx's theology is distinguished by its striking degree of intellectual depth and its authentic tone of moral urgency. His status as a quasi-public figure in Holland provides him with an opportunity, afforded only rarely to theologians, to practice the task of building bridges between Christianity and modern Western culture in the public arena. His abiding concern for contemporary mediations of the experience of God in Christ and his vision of the church as a participatory community of faith, based on more than a quarter of a century of experience in the Netherlands, helps to keep alive the hope that Vatican II inspired in many North American Catholics for a renewed church, a people of God. Drawing from the roots of this experience, he has reconceived theology as a form of reflection with intimate bonds to Christian living and dared to practice it that way on a scale unprecedented among male Catholic thinkers in the West. This approach to theology offers both a promise to ordinary believers and a challenge to theological colleagues in church and academy.

If such a theology remains sometimes more theoretical interpretation than historical praxis, or sometimes more political than mystical or vice versa, this should not appear unusual in a world that falls short of the kingdom of God. In the meantime, we who are both theologians and ordinary believers must have what Schillebeeckx calls the commitment to a historical praxis of mysticism and politics. In the midst of our daily tasks and our participation in the struggle for justice we can remember liturgically the story of Jesus' life, execution, and resurrection, to celebrate in thanksgiving the short-of-ultimate forms of salvation we have been given, and to hear, not in morbid guilt but in resolute trust, what Schillebeeckx has called "the gospel of the poor for prosperous people."

SUGGESTIONS FOR FURTHER READING

Schillebeeckx considers the methodological question explicitly in the sections of *Jesus* and *Christ* that reflect on interpretation and experience, and, in dialogue with his critics, in *Interim Report* and in his 1977 communication to the Congregation for the Doctrine of the Faith in Ted Schoof, ed., *The Schillebeeckx Case*. Required reading for anyone who would understand Schillebeeckx in his context in the Dutch Catholic experience is John A. Coleman's fascinating sociological study *The Evolution of Dutch Catholicism, 1958–1974* (Berkeley and Los Angeles: University of California Press, 1978), to which the above sketch is heavily indebted. The essays in *God the Future of Man* show Schillebeeckx appropriating secularization theology and hermeneutics. His little book *The Understanding of Faith* chronicles his dialogue with critical theory. In his two books *Ministry* and *The Church with a Human Face*, we find him engaging in theology as the critical reflection on Christian praxis. Part IV of the *Christ* book presents the most comprehensive treatment of Schillebeeckx's version of political theology. In public lectures from the same period such as the Erasmus Prize speech and the Abraham Kuyper lectures (*On Christian Faith: The Spiritual, Ethical and Political Dimensions*) he is working on a broader range of experiences and developing the categories of mysticism and politics.

3. Discovery of the Living God: Revelation and Experience

MARY CATHERINE HILKERT, O.P.

"Where is your God?" The question that haunted the psalmist confronts the secularized and suffering world of the late twentieth century with a new urgency. In a world in which science and technology can design the future of human beings and have the potential to destroy the planet, a transcendent God seems neither necessary nor credible and is, by definition, beyond empirical evidence. Further, the Christian hope in the promise of a future in which there will be "no more suffering and tears" is more vulnerable than ever to the charge of being mere illusion or more "opium for the people" in the face of Auschwitz, Hiroshima, Vietnam, and the continuing history of radical human suffering. Is it possible in that context to believe in a God "who casts no shadows on the world"? (*Understanding of Faith*, p. 100). Is there any point of contact in human experience for the preaching of a gospel that announces God's plan for humanity as a "future full of hope"? Can we speak with meaning of God's presence or God made known to humanity (revealed) in the contemporary world?

Long concerned with the fundamental pastoral question of the credibility of the Christian faith, Edward Schillebeeckx maintains that traces of the living God who is "the future of humanity" can be discovered in human experience—even in experiences of radical suffering. Modern theologians from Friedrich Schleiermacher, the father of liberal Protestantism, to the transcendental Thomist Karl Rahner have argued that God is to be found in the depths of human experience. On the contrary, dialectical theologians who have followed the lead of Karl Barth in facing squarely the realities of evil, suffering, and sin have insisted that the transcendent and hidden God is revealed only in the Word of God—

in Jesus the Christ, in the Scriptures, and in the church's proclamation of the gospel. In his recent writings, Schillebeeckx proposes a third possibility: God is revealed in human experience, but in a dialectical rather than a direct fashion. The ultimate mystery of compassion at the heart of reality surprises us as reality resists our human plans and expectations and as efforts on behalf of those who suffer disclose "something extra" in human experience: the absolute presence of the creator God.

Schillebeeckx's conviction that the encounter between God and humanity occurs within, but is not identical with, human experience involves a number of subtle and interrelated moves. He first locates the foundations for any discussion of revelation in an analysis of human experience and the relationship between experience and interpretation. In that context Schillebeeckx discusses the specifically religious experience of revelation, which can occur only within the horizon of a concrete faith tradition. His own Christian tradition further shapes Schillebeeckx's theology of revelation as he explores the Christian claim that God has been revealed uniquely in Jesus of Nazareth who is universal savior. Finally, Schillebeeckx explains that just as Christianity began with an experience of salvation (human wholeness rooted in an encounter with the living God in Jesus), the Christian tradition can be handed on only through a living history of discipleship. Human beings continue to encounter the living God in the concrete experience of their lives—or not at all. Following the movement of Schillebeeckx's thought we turn first to his discussion of human experience.

THE REVELATORY STRUCTURE OF
HUMAN EXPERIENCE

In his volume *Christ: The Experience of Jesus as Lord* Schillebeeckx introduces the opening discussion of revelation and experience by analyzing human growth and learning. Throughout life we develop through a process of exploration, risk, trial and error, and even failure. Human beings learn through experience. The frequently used term "experience" is not to be identified here with claims of personal preference or subjective feelings or emotional states. Rather, drawing on his philosophical background in phenomenology (see Chapters 1–2 above), Schillebeeckx explains that experience occurs as an encounter between a human subject and the givenness of reality in which objective and subjective elements are inextricably intertwined.

Because human beings are rational subjects this encounter with reality involves a reflective, a properly cognitive, dimension. We do not have raw human experience apart from some framework for understanding and perceiving. Rather, the ability to assimilate new perceptions is always related to a previous history of experiences—both personal and collective—that has resulted in one's present framework of interpretation. We interpret new experiences in the context of earlier experiences as they have developed into the traditions that now constitute our personal history, our family story, our religious heritage, or the various cultures and subcultures in which we live. Operating out of a basic preunderstanding (whether explicit or implicit), we are selective in our perception of reality. We notice or fail to notice new data. We attribute significance to actions and words. We experience new events from a specific perspective.

The very history of experience that forms one's interpretative horizon also serves to keep one open to new experiences. Truly experienced persons, Schillebeeckx notes, are the most open to new dimensions of reality as they integrate new moments of experience into an expanding sphere of reference. He emphasizes that this "subjective sphere of resonance" does not preclude an objective dimension to experience. On the contrary, one's expanding horizon, guided by critical reflection on past experience, makes one more open to encounter reality in its givenness. The trained musician, Schillebeeckx reminds us, hears more dimensions in a symphony than does a person with an untrained ear.

The interplay here between perception and thought is constant and subtle. New experience is possible only within an interpretative horizon, but one's framework of previously developed models and concepts is constantly corrected, changed, and revised in light of new and unexpected encounters. Frequently reality resists our expectations and forces us to "think again." At times our encounters with reality confirm or verify our human projections, but more often, Schillebeeckx suggests, we learn by way of discovery. Hence Schillebeeckx describes new experience as both *critical* (it calls into question inherited insights and previous frameworks) and *productive* (it evokes new and unexpected ways of perceiving and deeper levels of reflection, meaning, and action.) The cognitive dimension of experience is crucial here. The initially projected framework and critical reflection are part of the experience itself. Human beings have to make conjectures, form hypotheses, and experiment if reality is to be encountered, but the experience itself calls us to rethink our models, to confirm, revise, or reject our hypotheses.

Eventually, this self-correcting process of learning can result in a fundamental paradigm shift in which a radically new framework for perceiving reality is necessary if we are to understand adequately the data of new experience. We are familiar with this process of radical conversion in moments of scientific discovery. Einstein's theory of relativity, for example, provided a framework for understanding the universe that could account for evidence inexplicable within the horizon of Newton's laws of nature.

Schillebeeckx argues that new experience carries a claim to authority particularly when it fails to confirm previous expectations: "Truth comes near to us by the alienation and disorientation of what we have already achieved and planned" (*Christ*, p. 35). Experiences that are continuous with our previous framework of interpretation may or may not find their source in a reality beyond our projections and hopes. The very refractory character of discontinuous or surprising experiences is the best guarantee of a revelation of reality that surpasses our imagination and control. Schillebeeckx asserts that "People learn from failures—where their projects are blocked and they make a new attempt, in sensitive reverence for the resistance and thus for the orientation of reality" (*Christ*, p. 35). Failures remind us that we are finite. We do not define or control reality; rather reality sustains and guides us.

One of Schillebeeckx's most perduring convictions (drawn from his phenomenological background) that proves crucial to his theology of revelation emerges at this point: experience contains a dimension of "givenness" that comes from beyond the subject. While there is no uninterpreted experience, neither can experience be reduced to the subjective construct or creation of the interpreter. Reality remains independent of the perceiver—something we cannot manipulate or change. While reality is encountered only as perceived, fundamental elements of interpretation are given in the experience. Still, these "primary elements of interpretation" cannot be distinguished neatly from the subjective interpretative framework of the experiencing subject. Schillebeeckx uses the experience of love (which has, he notes, a close connection with the experience of grace) to illustrate this interpenetration of experience and interpretation. Interpretation based on prior experiences of love is involved in the very act of experiencing a new relationship as "love." Later the experience may be expressed in language taken from literature (e.g., Romeo and Juliet), the Scriptures (e.g., the Song of Songs or 1 Cor 13), or various cultural descriptions of love. These interpretative expressions of the experience both deepen the experience and well up from the experience itself.

Exploring further the connections between experience, interpretation, and expression, Schillebeeckx concludes that human experience has a narrative structure. One who has had an experience with some power to disclose reality (an authoritative experience) spontaneously wants to express what has happened. Experience is communicated primarily through word—we share our experiences by telling stories. Traditions, formed from collective experience, become the social framework for understanding—the common stories of families, communities, and cultures. Narration opens up the possibility of sharing in a new story. Through narrative one is able to offer others the possibility of a new "experience with experiences."

On the other hand, new experience or new narratives do not *necessarily* carry the authority of reality confronting us with new truth. Rather, experienced persons and communities exercise critical reflection and judgment as they incorporate new facets of experience into their "living traditions." This very capacity of discerning judgment develops as the result of a history of experience and previously critically digested perceptions. Further, while the disclosure of new experience involves a process of disintegration and transformation prior to a fully reoriented reintegration, the discovery of the new is also in some sense a rediscovery. Because we are a part of the reality that reveals itself to us, the alienation that results from the unexpected brings the new element in experience into view as something that is somewhat familiar even if beyond all previous expectations.

While Schillebeeckx argues that human experience has a revelatory structure (we learn by discovery), not all human experiences are equally revelatory. Rather, in the midst of our ordinary daily lives certain events and experiences provide a point of breakthrough, even cause a kind of "gestalt switch" in the way we live and understand ourselves and life (radical conversion). Whether suddenly or gradually, something surprising happens in which, upon reflection, we recognize deeper dimensions of ourselves and of reality. Even a smile or a friendly glance, Schillebeeckx observes, can open a new world for us. Further, there are radical experiences of "limit" or "boundary" in life, experiences of contingency and finitude in which the fundamental question of the meaning of human life emerges. These boundaries of human experience are reached both in experiences that overflow with a "surplus of meaning" that cannot be expressed in ordinary secular language and in the negative experiences of human suffering, injustice, and ultimately death. In depth experiences of meaning and in the struggle with the "pain of contrast" in experiences of apparent meaninglessness, human beings experience reality as a whole either as ultimately absurd or as fundamentally trustworthy. In these "disclosure experiences" a deeper dimension of reality unfolds. As Schillebeeckx describes them, experiences at the limits of human life "cry out for integration" in the context of reality as a whole.

THE RELIGIOUS EXPERIENCE OF REVELATION AND THE HORIZON OF FAITH

It is precisely here, at the depths or boundaries of the human situation, that the specifically religious experience of revelation is available as a new "experience with experiences." Here Schillebeeckx emphasizes that religious experience is not a special feeling or a direct experience of the divine; rather, most fundamentally, it is an experience of the graciousness of reality as a whole. In the existential experience of human finitude something deeper is disclosed and evoked: "The experience of reality as a gift which frees us from the impossible attempt to find a basis in ourselves" (*Christ*, p. 47).

Not only positive experiences that disclose an ultimate ground to human meaning, but even negative or "contrast experiences" reveal a fundamental affirmation undergirding human experience. As early as 1967 Schillebeeckx had adopted the term "contrast experience" to describe those experiences of negativity (on both personal and social levels) that evoke both protest and hope on behalf of humanity. In spite of radical pluralism and disagreement about what constitutes humanity and human happiness, Schillebeeckx remarks that we know, in at least a negative way, what violates humanity. Situations of evil and injustice trigger the spontaneous response: "No, it can't go on like this, we won't stand for it any longer" (*God the Future of Man*, p. 136). As human beings respond to experiences of evil, injustice, and suffering with hope, endurance, protest, and resistance, something beyond human finitude is disclosed. "Something extra" sustains humanity stretched to its limits. Both positive disclosure experiences and negative "contrast experiences" form the foundation in human experience that grounds the religious claim that there is a mystery of graciousness at the depth of human experience and of reality as a whole, the mystery believers identify as "the divine" or name "God."

Ultimately, Schillebeeckx suggests, "in our experiences we can *experience* something that transcends our experience and proclaims itself in that experience as unexpected grace" (*Christ*, p. 78). Since revelation in the religious sense refers to the manifestation of the divine within the human, the eschatological within the historical, it cannot be discovered in a direct appeal to self-evident experience. Rather, reflection is demanded if we are to recognize the call that summons us beyond the limits we have taken for granted. Describing this "transcendence within immanence," Schillebeeckx calls revelation "the crossing of a boundary within the dimensions of human existence" (*Christ*, p. 62). Here it is important to note that Schillebeeckx locates revelation as occurring within human experience, but also that the two are not identical—revelation involves crossing a boundary. There is a dimension of givenness "from above" or "from beyond"—the specifically transcendent dimension (the experience*d*) in revelatory experience.

Here Schillebeeckx clearly distinguishes his position from both the modernist identification of revelation with human experience in its depths and the neoscholastic understanding of revelation in terms of a propositional "deposit of faith" contained in Scripture and tradition (largely identified with church teachings). Even in his early work contained in the two-volume *Revelation and Theology*, Schillebeeckx distinguished between "revelation-in-reality" (the encounter between God and humanity that occurs in human history and definitively in Jesus) and "revelation-in-word" (the necessarily limited and historically conditioned conceptual expressions of that mystery). God's gracious self-offer to humanity always transcends human understanding and expression.

In his earlier writings Schillebeeckx described the encounter between God and humanity as a dialogue in which God's self-offer constituted revelation and faith was identified with the human response. In recent writings, however, he draws an even closer connection between revelation and faith. The very experience of reality as grounded in a transcendent dimension of graciousness (as well as the further claim that the divine is personal or that God has been revealed definitively in Jesus Christ) occurs only in the context of some sort of tradition of faith. Hence Schillebeeckx describes revelation as God's saving action in history "as *experienced* by believers and *interpreted* in religious language and therefore expressed in human terms, in the dimension of our utterly human history" (*Christ*, p. 78).

While revelation as God's initiative in the divine-human encounter always grounds the human response of faith, the offer is completed and recognized only in the response. Revelation is not an objective "given" that historically precedes a later subjective "response"; rather, revelation occurs only within the horizon of faith. Based on the convictions that there is no uninterpreted experience and revelation occurs within human experience, Schillebeeckx remarks that the believer and the nonbeliever *experience* reality differently. Faith is not merely an interpretation that can be applied retrospectively to one's previously neutral (uninterpreted) experiences. Rather, faith is the horizon within which the believer perceives reality and experiences human life. Hence Schillebeeckx concludes that "the religious person experiences grace [and] does not just interpret it" (*Christ*, p. 54).

Borrowing a term from linguistic analysts, Schillebeeckx describes faith as an alternative "language game" through which secular human history is interpreted (and thus experienced) according to the "grammar of hope." Religious language points to the disclosure of God's creative presence precisely within human experience. Speaking at the limits of experience as described in profane or scientific language, the believer dares to utter a further word. Especially in Western cultures where science and technology propose the dominant values, a large part of reality falls outside the horizon of possible human experience. Expressions of protest emerge in the aesthetic, the contemplative, the playful, the spontaneous, and ultimately the religious. One of the important functions of the language of faith is simply to keep open the question and possibility of transcendence in a radically secular world.

The alternative vision of faith (and thus the experience of God's self-offer) can be expressed only metaphorically and symbolically since faith claims to speak about a depth dimension of reality that is unavailable to conceptual and rational thought. Only the evocative language of faith can render the substance and meaning of the disclosure experiences that occur at the limits of human experience open and comprehensible to others. As witnesses tell the story of their experience of grace, a social frame of reference is created and transmitted. The story of faith becomes an invitation to others to share the experience of human life in light of faith.

Here Schillebeeckx is careful to remind his readers that the history of salvation (or God's liberating love) cannot be identified with the history of revelation or religious experience (which involves an explicit awareness of God's saving action). There are many kinds of interpretative experiences of salvation. Within a religious tradition of experience, however, human liberation is seen in relation to God—its heart and source. Each religious tradition offers a unique framework ("search pattern") within which believers experience human history in relation to the divine. Just as all experience occurs only in the context of a specific framework of interpretation, religious experience occurs only in the context of specific religious traditions. Thus the variety of religious traditions in the world provides multiple possibilities for a religious experience of human life.

THE CHRISTIAN CLAIM:
GOD REVEALED UNIQUELY IN JESUS

Granting that the living God of all creation is present "wherever good is promoted and evil fought" and that God is encountered and worshiped within multiple traditions of faith, Schillebeeckx develops his theology of revelation within the interpretative framework of his own faith tradition—Christianity. Christians claim that who God is and how God wills to be experienced has been shown by God in the historical encounter with Jesus of Nazareth and in the history that led up to that event. God's love for humanity has been revealed in a special way in the life, ministry, death, and resurrection of Jesus of Nazareth. The Christian story, as Schillebeeckx frequently repeats, "began with an experience." In Jesus, the disciples encountered something more: "salvation coming from God." Standing within the interpretative framework of the Jewish faith—specifically Israel's dream of the reign of God as human salvation—the disciples experienced something new that both fulfilled and far exceeded their expectations. They experienced the presence of God in their midst in a radically new way in the preaching, liberating life-style, death, and resurrection of Jesus.

In their expression of their Easter experience ("I have seen the Lord") as well as in later expressions of the experience of salvation (redemption, justification, forgiveness of sins, and so forth) or in the names they gave Jesus (e.g., the Christ, Messiah, Lord, Son of God), the earliest Christians spoke in language drawn from their social-cultural milieu and religious traditions. But limited human expressions always "break up under the pressure of what Jesus really was, said, and did" (*Interim Report*, p. 26). Resistant reality, now recognized, named, and experienced as God in Jesus continued to break open limited human expectations and expressions.

While even the original expressions of faith cannot communicate the fullness of the mystery experienced, the faith of later generations of Christian believers remains dependent on the historical mediation of the experiences of faith of earlier generations of Christian believers. In a unique way the "source experience" of faith of the apostolic community is essential to the faith of all believers in the tradition, since it was the first generation of believers who encountered Jesus historically and who experienced, both in his life and in the new disclosure of the Easter event, definitive salvation coming from God.

The apostolic experience of salvation became a message—the *kerygma*—that extended the possibility of living the Christian life to others. Hence the question of whether faith derives from experience or "faith comes from hearing" poses a false dilemma according to Schillebeeckx. The Christian message began as an experience, but the experience of salvation that took place in the concrete history and resurrection of Jesus is available to later generations only if the disciples of Jesus continue to hand on the Christian story in a living tradition that "in words and actions bridges the gulf between us and what happened then" (*Interim Report*, p. 7).

LIVING TRADITION: THE TRANSMISSION OF FAITH

This notion of living tradition is central to Schillebeeckx's understanding of revelation. Tradition, he explains, is constituted by a history of vital experience: "What was experience for others yesterday is tradition for us today, and what is experience for us today will in turn be tradition for others tomorrow" (*Interim Report*, p. 50). Influenced by Yves Congar's distinction between tradition and traditions, Schillebeeckx had noted already in his early writings on "revelation and its tradition" that the "deposit of faith" entrusted to the church and handed on from apostolic times is the entire "mystery of Christ," not only formulations about or teachings of Jesus. Fundamentally, the living Christian tradition is constituted by the Holy Spirit active in and through communities of Christian discipleship.

No one creates the Christian story anew or discovers Jesus in an unmediated fashion. Rather, contemporary believers have been offered the testimony of earlier witnesses of faith in the ongoing movement that Jesus initiated and the Spirit sustains. Any tradition continues to exist as a vital reality, however, only insofar as it is able to address and incorporate new cultures and historical situations within its history. The "culture shock" that results when earlier cultural expressions of the gospel no longer convey the critical and productive force of the Christian faith is, according to Schillebeeckx, a necessary "life shock" calling forth new expressions of the gospel so that it might become a universal historical message of salvation.

The transmission of the Christian tradition in every age and culture requires far more than the repetition of the *kerygma* or doctrinal formulations. A living tradition of faith, Schillebeeckx insists, demands a true "updating" that puts the gospel message into operation in the present day in the face of "completely new experiences which are themselves foreign to the Bible" (*Jesus*, p. 753). Schillebeeckx's consistent interest in hermeneutics (see Chapters 1–2 above) has been prompted by the danger that culturally antiquated formulations of the Christian faith, rather than the demands of the gospel, will become the stumbling block to contemporary believers. Even the biblical texts that mediate salvation in Jesus as experienced by the earliest Christian communities and thus provide the "inescapable and historically reliable point of departure for the Christian tradition" (*Jesus*, p. 44) remain nonetheless the culturally and historically conditioned expressions of a movement that has continued in the Spirit of the risen Jesus and that must be reexpressed uniquely in every cultural context. Similarly, the later doctrinal formulations of the Christian faith, while essential to a living tradition that is mediated through history, cannot be identified with the deeper mystery to which they point—the experience of revelation. The gospel's claim to universal significance becomes credible only if the proclamation of faith can be reinterpreted and reactualized in every new cultural situation.

Ultimately the gospel promises that the mystery of God is active in human history on behalf of human well-being. The claim that at the depth of reality is the God who is "bent upon humanity" cannot be reinterpreted and transmitted in a purely theoretical fashion. It must be proved true in the lives of discipleship (faith praxis) of communities of believers who strive to make the promise of salvation a concrete reality in the contemporary world. The hope that at the heart of reality is the God whose true name is compassion is both "too much" for humanity to grasp (an eschatological reality within the confines of human history) and "too little" for humans to understand (the absurdity of evil is utterly unintelligible; the non-sense of history is resistant to theorizing). Hence theoretical expressions of faith (which Schillebeeckx had always admitted were limited in their ability to express the inexhaustible mystery of the encounter between God and humanity) break down in their ability to transmit the mystery of revelation in history. The "scarlet counterthreads" of human suffering in the fabric of human history stand in irreconcilable contrast to any claims of universal theoretical meaning to human history.

The Christian belief that the meaning of universal history is to be found in the life story of Jesus becomes a living tradition only when that story is retold in the lives of his followers. Contemporary believers can preach God's fierce opposition to human suffering only if they preach as Jesus did—in person and action as well as in word. Proclamation of redemption in the face of all the evidence to the contrary requires living remembrance of the crucified Jesus, who in the midst of radical historical failure remained faithful to the One he knew as *Abba* and whose hope was justified in the resurrection. Remembrance in the biblical sense (*anamnesis*) is a living remembrance through action in the present. Without some experience of the truth of the gospel proclamation, the "Word of God" is not only a metaphor—it is sheer illusion.

While ethical action carries what Schillebeeckx calls the "greatest density of revelation" (since it makes God's promise concretely present in history in real though fragmentary ways), Christian praxis and Christian proclamation mutually interpret one another. Proclamation without praxis becomes ideology, but praxis without proclamation loses the orientation and critical force of the gospel. Here Schillebeeckx highlights the revelatory power, the practical and critical effect, in narrative. Stories forged in human experience have the power to touch and transform the human experience of others. Specifically in the context of human suffering, narrative has the further power of retrieving the history of those whose lives have been forgotten, the invisible characters in the human story who have been dismissed as insignificant. Narrative and praxis are integrally related because remembrance of past human suffering carries an implicit ethical demand—it becomes a stimulus for liberating action. At a new moment in the tradition new responses to the gospel imperative are demanded; "new memories" of Jesus are discovered.

Because of the sustaining and empowering presence of the Holy Spirit within the Christian community there is a continual interaction between remembering and later experience. Recalling the Johannine promise that "the Spirit will bring all things to remembrance" (Jn 14:26; 15:26; 16:13–14), Schillebeeckx maintains that the "new memories" of the Christian community are no less authentic expressions of revelation simply because they are new. Rather, precisely because Christian revelation occurs as interpreted experience within human history, the contemporary reactualization of the tradition (in praxis and narrative) participates not only in the transmission, but also in the creation of the living tradition of faith.

MUTUALLY CRITICAL CORRELATION OF APOSTOLIC AND CONTEMPORARY EXPERIENCES OF FAITH

While new expressions of the Christian tradition must be forged in every unique historical situation, it is precisely because of their claim to reactualize the gospel of Jesus that the contemporary proclamation and praxis of the church must be held in a mutually critical correlation with the rest of the tradition (and in a particular way with the originating moment of the tradition in the "phenomenon of Jesus"). Authentic updating of the Christian tradition must be at once "creative" and "true to Jesus" (*Jesus*, p. 753).

Hence Schillebeeckx grants that the New Testament has an irreplaceable and unique role in the Christian tradition since it mediates contact with the apostolic faith experience, the primary response to Jesus as God's self-offer in history. Thus it gives "the most direct, uniquely practicable and historically reliable access to the original event, the Christian movement that took its impetus from Jesus of Nazareth" (*Jesus*, p. 58).

The apostolic faith is mediated in history, however, only if Christian experience continues to be a viable option in later generations and in other cultures. There is no abstract Christian faith; there is only the faith as made concretely available in communities of Christian believers. Hence the Christian tradition, like all human experience, is mediated necessarily through social and political structures. Reflecting on the insights of critical theorists (see chapters 1–2 above), Schillebeeckx recognized the danger here: the necessary historical mediation of the gospel in human structures and language may distort the very tradition it is attempting to transmit. Human history is a "flesh and blood affair," Schillebeeckx reminds us; in includes sin as well as grace, unconscious as well as conscious elements of interpretation. False concepts and repressive structures that benefit a dominant group emerge in the power struggles of human history, including the human history of the church. Unless a critical perspective on the Christian tradition is maintained, untruths or non-sense can be consciously or unconsciously legitimated by those in power to preserve their own interests.

Still Schillebeeckx remains convinced that the living tradition of faith will transcend every ideological formulation and will break through all repressive processes and structures since the Holy Spirit is the ultimate subject and guarantor of the Christian tradition. A necessary critical perspective on the Christian tradition emerges ultimately, according to Schillebeeckx, from the liberating and critical character of the gospel itself. The prophetic Spirit of God destroys idols and breaks open human frameworks of interpretation that limit or distort the revelation of the mystery of God.

Recognizing revelation within human experience becomes the task of "discerning the Spirit" active in the process of the living Christian tradition. Discovering the authority of revelation located in human experience is a complex phenomenon that requires critical reflection. The authority of revelation cannot be identified solely with the apostolic expression of faith or with any particular later mediation of the "great Christian tradition" including contemporary new enculturations of Christian faith. Rather, locating the authority of revelation in human experience requires a mutually critical correlation of tradition and new experience.

The story of Jesus made available to us through the New Testament does not simply confirm contemporary human experience. Every epoch and culture has its own unique sensitivities, but also its biases and limitations. Hence every age and culture has access to unique aspects of revelation, but each culture also has its own possibilities for distortion of the tradition. The apostolic experience of faith as expressed in the New Testament critiques our limited and sinful perspectives on the basis of the memory of Jesus and the vision of the reign of God he proclaimed. The critical question that confronts present enculturations of the Christian faith (e.g., experiments in liturgy or ministry) that claim to be creative yet faithful actualizations of the gospel in a new time is: to what extent is the historical identity of Christianity made present in a new way and to what extent is it compromised or distorted in this new praxis or expression of the tradition?

Schillebeeckx also notes, however, that the apostolic and traditional formulations of revelation must be critiqued from the perspective of contemporary experience. Recognizing that some may consider it blasphemous to assert that the "Word of God" can be criticized by human experience, Schillebeeckx hastens to point out that it is our human speaking about the Word of God that is in need of evaluation. Again the complex structure of experiences of revelation becomes apparent. Revelation never occurs as pure "Word of God"; it occurs in "utterly human history" as interpreted in the context of a specific tradition of faith and as expressed in culturally limited language. Differing cultural vantage points offer the possibility of identifying the limitations of other enculturations of the gospel. The ultimate theological reason for the necessity of critique of the Christian tradition from the perspective of "a new moment in the tradition" is that the historical church can never be absolutely identified with Jesus Christ. The power of God revealed in the resurrection can open up new possibilities, create a future that exceeds past hopes and memories and present expectations and limits.

While the Holy Spirit may indeed be "doing a new thing" at a new moment in history, Schillebeeckx still cautions that the Holy Spirit is the Spirit of Jesus. The Christian tradition has its norm in its fidelity to Jesus. Hence new moments in the tradition must also establish their fidelity to "the great Christian tradition." Discovering the living God in the history of human experience requires a careful process of "discernment of the Spirit" as contemporary communities of believers, in fidelity to Jesus and the apostolic tradition, strive to share the experience of revelation with others by "writing a fifth gospel with their lives."

SUGGESTIONS FOR FURTHER READING

Schillebeeckx's most extended treatment (in English) of the relationship between revelation and experience is to be found in *Christ: The Experience of Jesus as Lord* pp. 29–79. Briefer versions of his key insights on this topic are available in *Interim Report on the Books "Jesus" and "Christ"* pp. 3-19, 50–63; and "Can Christology Be an Experiment?" in *Proceedings of the Catholic Theological Society of America* 35 (1980): 1–14. The first chapter of *On Christian Faith* provides his most recent discussion of the relationship between God and the world.

The fullest development of the topics discussed in this chapter is located in Schillebeeckx's (as yet) untranslated article "Erfahrung und Glaube," in *Christlicher Glaube in moderner Gesellschaft,* Teilband 25 (Freiburg: Herder, 1980), pp. 73–116.

For the early roots of Schillebeeckx's theology of revelation see his *Revelation and Theology* vols. 1 and 2, (New York: Sheed and Ward, 1967, 1968). Parts I and II of *The Schillebeeckx Reader* provide an excellent introduction to Schillebeeckx's contemporary understanding of the relationship between experience and revelation as well as the development of his theology of revelation.

4. Retelling the Story of Jesus: Christology

JOHN P. GALVIN

In an influential programmatic essay, "Current Problems in Christology," originally published in 1954, the German Jesuit theologian Karl Rahner lamented the failure of contemporary Catholic theologians to address anew central christological issues. Literature abounded in other areas, Rahner noted, such as the theology of grace and even mariology, and debates raged concerning such topics as the extent of Christ's human knowledge and the precise nature of the hypostatic union. But a general presumption prevailed among Catholic theologians that the decisive, foundational issues of christology had long since been resolved. In the fourth and fifth centuries, ecumenical councils at Nicaea, Ephesus, and Chalcedon had settled matters concerning the person of Christ by teaching definitively that Jesus Christ is truly God and truly human, one person (divine) in two natures (divine and human). In the Middle Ages, St. Anselm of Canterbury had developed the account of Christ's work that soon became standard in Western thought: in his death on the cross Christ had freely offered himself to God as infinite satisfaction for human sin. The task of christology was to repeat and defend these established teachings, not to reexamine their bases or expand the field of inquiry to include broader questions.

In Rahner's judgment, this widespread presumption was wrong. Without denying the validity of the conciliar formula or the value of the traditional theory of satisfaction, he argued that a host of other problems urgently required attention, foremost among them issues arising from recent biblical studies and from the pastoral need to rearticulate central convictions of Christian faith with a view to the specific concerns of modernity. The formulations of the past were starting points as well as conclusions. The task of christology was not simply one of conserving the received tradition; it included as well an obligation to retrieve from the past the memory of forgotten truths and a duty to address creatively new questions and problems.

While the accuracy of Rahner's diagnosis was widely acknowledged, the christological program he envisioned was not pursued immediately. In the following years, the energies of most theologians were absorbed by issues concerning the church and the sacraments—the major themes on the agenda of the Second Vatican Council (1962–1965). Since the early 1970s, however, it has become increasingly clear that confronting the challenges faced by Christianity in the modern world necessitates fundamental reexamination of central aspects of the church's faith; as a result, christology has occupied center stage in theological discussion. Rahner himself summarized much of his thought on christology in an important section of *Foundations of Christian Faith*. Hans Küng devoted over half of *On Being a Christian* to a presentation of christological themes, and Walter Kasper published a comprehensive textbook on christology, *Jesus the Christ*. In addition to these major books, numerous studies have examined individual christological questions or provided introductory accounts of modern christology on a more popular level.

Among these many recent works, Edward Schillebeeckx's massive christological project clearly holds a prominent place. Schillebeeckx has addressed christology from a distinctive perspective that sheds fresh light on the topics he examines. In addition, more than any other contemporary systematic theologian, he has elaborated his christological thought in detailed engagement with the writings of recent biblical scholars. As we shall see, the result is an intriguing—and provocative—retelling of the story of Jesus as a story of God.

THE PROBLEM OF EVIL AND THE OPTION
FOR NARRATIVE

Schillebeeckx's christology begins with a problem, not a formula or a theory. His quest for a suitable starting point common to all human life and therefore accessible to all leads him to concentrate on the universal experience of evil, the bitter awareness that the history of the human race is a history of suffering. Without disparaging the significance of other concerns, Schillebeeckx remains convinced that the problem of evil, concretized most disturbingly in the suffering of the innocent, is both the primary issue that has preoccupied religions and philosophies of the past and present and the most urgent challenge faced by Christianity today.

Needed in response to the presence of evil is not an explanation of its existence or a theory about its origin or purpose. The point is not to interpret the world differently, but to change it. In themselves, neither explanations nor theories offer helpful solutions. On the contrary, they can easily prove counterproductive, as they may suggest that evil is inevitable, ineradicably rooted in the order of things, and thus promote an attitude of resignation and passivity. For these reasons, Schillebeeckx maintains, the problem of evil is not amenable to theoretical argument or resolution.

Rather than theory, the proper reaction to evil is concrete opposition to its reign; "the only adequate response is via a practical exercise of resistance to evil, not a theory about it" (*Jesus*, p. 620). But this resistance, in turn, is in need of support; otherwise, in the face of intractable and deep-seated problems, it will surely prove ineffective and short-lived. Here widespread human practice offers a sure guide: "Peole do not *argue* against suffering, but tell a *story*" (*Christ*, p. 698). At the root of such stories lie contrast experiences, in which we grasp the tension between the general sway of injustice and our fleeting achievement of meaning and reconciliation. Unlike theories, which tend to domesticate problems and thus to perpetuate them, the telling and retelling of stories preserves dangerous memories, awakens liberating hopes, and provides a framework for expressing specific anticipations of a better future in parables and symbols—the only suitable vehicles of communication in a world where evil still abounds. In view of the pervasive problem of suffering, discourse is necessary, and the appropriate primary form for discourse is that of a narrative with practical intent.

But the selection of a story cannot be arbitrary, and the right story is hard to find. In the judgment of Christians, the story to be told in the face of evil is christological. To tell this story today, in view of contemporary perceptions of concerns to be addressed and of modern standards for proper historical narrative, is a particularly demanding task. Yet it is this project that Schillebeeckx has undertaken, for his understanding of the problem that theology must confront both necessitates a pursuit of christological issues and dictates his choice of christological method. As a result, his christology does not concentrate on a christological formula—not even the hallowed formula of the Council of Chalcedon. Nor does it develop a soteriological theory—not even the traditional theory of Christ's atoning sacrifice. Fully aware how hard it is to tell a story well, yet firmly oriented on the narrative form of the gospels, Schillebeeckx instead attempts to retell the life story of Jesus as a liberating story of God.

NARRATIVE AND EXEGESIS

As Schillebeeckx recognizes, "the starting point of the Christian movement was an indissoluble whole consisting on the one hand of the offer of salvation through Jesus and on the other of the Christian response in faith" (*Christ*, p. 66). While discussion of Jesus requires particular attention to the first aspect of this composite—to "those features of the 'historical Jesus' which may have led to the New Testament confession of him" (*Christ*, p. 22)—our historical access to Jesus remains mediated through the prism of the responses he evoked from others. To reach the Jesus of history, it is necessary to retrace one's way through the Gospels, which are composed from the perspectives of their early Christian authors yet enshrine earlier historical material. This, in turn, demands careful consideration of the issues raised by modern historical-critical scrutiny of the New Testament.

Thus, to accomplish his goal of retelling the story of Jesus, Schillebeeckx had to immerse himself thoroughly in contemporary exegetical literature. Though not a professional exegete, he has attained sufficient mastery of the literature and methods of exegesis to enable him to pass well-informed judgments on biblical questions. While his perspective remains that of a systematic theologian, his presentation of Jesus bears witness to the depth of his exegetical studies and provides a valuable summary of recent New Testament research.

In pursuing these issues, Schillebeeckx proposes five criteria helpful for distinguishing what may actually be ascribed to the historical Jesus from subsequent amplifications by the early church: the presence of material that diverges from the theological tendencies of the work in which it appears; the existence of material that cannot plausibly be attributed to sources other than Jesus; the presence of the same material in diverse traditions; consistency in content between a given detail and the overall picture of Jesus; and, finally, the standard of Jesus' execution—Jesus' life must be such that it accounts for his rejection and death. Application of these criteria, in wide-ranging dialogue with modern biblical scholarship, allows him to provide an unusually rich and detailed account of Jesus' public life.

JESUS' PUBLIC LIFE

Schillebeeckx presents Jesus' public life as a sustained and varied offer of definitive salvation from God in a context marked by intense suffering and correspondingly heightened longings. Jesus' joyful gospel of God's graciousness—clearly distinguishable from John the Baptist's somber message of divine judgment, despite the two prophets' common stress on hope and ethical commitment—is expressed in both his preaching and his conduct.

Jesus' preaching was addressed to all Israel and concentrated on the theme of God's kingdom, of God's benevolent rule. What Jesus meant by the term "kingdom of God" emerges from his ministry as a whole, not from direct explanation on his part. His open-ended parables interrupt the course of events, forcing his listeners to think further and revealing through their effects what God is like. His enunciation of the Beatitudes (a core of which derives from Jesus himself) shows him as the bearer of good tidings to the poor. Throughout his preaching, Jesus indicates as a present reality God's radical "no" to all forms of evil, for the kingdom, which Jesus announces the imminent arrival of, is in fact at hand in Jesus himself.

The same liberating message is embodied in Jesus' prophetic life, for his company was experienced as the presence of God's saving rule. His activity as healer and exorcist, though difficult to document in detail, evoked an incipient faith in the sense of a turning of people toward him. Table fellowship with him, and even more the common life of his chosen disciples, communicated a sense of well-being and freedom in his presence. In sum, Jesus not only used parables to speak about God; he was himself in an even deeper sense God's own parable of mercy and liberation.

Yet Schillebeeckx's probing of Jesus' life does not rest content with a summary of what Jesus said and did. In his judgment, it is necessary even on purely historical grounds to inquire into the unifying source of Jesus' message and conduct. Anything less would mark a failure to recognize the extent to which the mystery of Jesus' person is indirectly accessible to us in and through his behavior, a blindness to the fact that while Jesus never placed himself beside God's kingdom as a second topic in his preaching, still "his person is never entirely separable from his message and ministry" (*Jesus*, p. 258). The inseparability of Jesus' message from his person is a central factor in Schillebeeckx's christology.

Schillebeeckx locates the foundation of Jesus' activity in his consciousness of deep intimacy with God, who benevolently opposes evil and refuses to allow it to have the last word. Jesus' message and manner of life reflect a confident hope that cannot have been grounded in the calamitous history of the world. Their only possible source lies in an intuitive grasp, on Jesus' part, of the sharp contrast between the evil he observed and his personal experience of God.

As a brief capsulation of this abiding awareness at the heart of Jesus' ministry, Schillebeeckx has coined the term "*Abba* experience." Originating from the Aramaic word for "father," the term is based on Jesus' frequent reference to God as Father in the Gospels and especially on the use of the Aramaic word *Abba* (in Greek transliteration) in three New Testament texts (Mk 14:36, Rom 8:15; Gal 4:6). Yet Schillebeeckx's insistence that a conviction of intimacy with God lies at the source of Jesus' public activity rests on an overall consideration of Jesus' life and message, not on an exegesis of the passages in which the word "father" appears. His choice of language simply reflects, in terminology rooted in the New Testament, the loving proximity and trust that characterized Jesus' relationship with God.

As Schillebeeckx recognizes clearly, these considerations in themselves do not establish the validity of Jesus' claim. Historical investigations alone cannot determine whether his *Abba* experience was well founded or illusory. But they do show that, in this case, the message and the messenger are inseparable. For this reason, any effort to assess the truth of what Jesus proclaimed will ultimately find it necessary to weigh the consequences Jesus faced for having advanced his gospel.

THE CRUCIFIXION

The stark fact of Jesus' crucifixion inevitably raises questions for any theologian, and it does so with particular urgency for Schillebeeckx, who accents so strongly the salvific impact of Jesus' presence. His narrative treatment of the subject includes an examination of Jesus' approach to death and an analysis of early Christian interpretations of the crucifixion; in addition, he offers his own reflections on the theological meaning of the cross. Each of these three aspects deserves separate consideration.

JESUS' APPROACH TO DEATH

Aware that texts in the gospels are often formulated from the perspective of the early church, modern treatments of Jesus' approach to death understandably hesitate to rely on biblical passages in which Jesus discusses in advance his own death. While a few scholars, such as Rudolf Bultmann, doubt that we are able to determine at all how Jesus faced death, Schillebeeckx follows the more moderate consensus that Jesus, long aware of potential danger from many hostile forces, gradually achieved certitude of impending violence. His steadfast adherence to his mission under these adverse circumstances implies on his part acceptance of death as a consequence of continued fidelity to his ministry. The early church was thus justified in its unanimous attestation "that Jesus went to the cross freely and deliberately" (*Jesus*, p. 302).

In arguing this position, Schillebeeckx stresses that a decisive break in the public evaluation of Jesus occurred well before his death, at the point where mounting opposition to his message coalesced into the personal rejection that eventually culminated in his crucifixion. Aware of this reaction and conscious as well of the tension between his approaching execution and his message of God's kingdom, Jesus must have pondered the meaning of the death he was to undergo. In view of this situation, it is possible and legitimate to ask if Jesus not only accepted his death freely, but also provided for his disciples an advance interpretation of its significance.

In addressing this issue, Schillebeeckx proceeds quite cautiously. On the one hand, he appeals to a critically reliable text in the Last Supper tradition ("Truly I say to you, I shall not drink again of the fruit of the vine until that day when I drink it new in the kingdom of God" [Mt 14:25]) to argue that, even face to face with death, Jesus confidently retained unbroken assurance of eventual salvation and vindication. On the other hand, holding that we have no certainly authentic passage in which Jesus ascribes salvific value to his death, he suggests that Jesus left his death as a final prophetic sign for others to interpret on the basis of his life. In any case, Jesus' fidelity in life and death to his gospel of salvation far surpasses in importance any theoretical reconciliation of his message and his fate.

EARLY CHRISTIAN INTERPRETATIONS OF THE CRUCIFIXION

Continuing his narrative presentation to include the reflections of the early church, Schillebeeckx draws on the work of numerous exegetes to outline three major early Christian interpretations of the crucifixion: Jesus' death was seen as the death of the eschatological prophet-martyr, as the death of the righteous sufferer, and as a redemptive, atoning death. These interpretations, which antedate the writing of the New Testament, may well have developed simultaneously in different Christian communities.

One line of thought readily accessible to early Christians accented Jesus' prophetic life and drew on the Old Testament theme that true prophets are often rejected and meet a violent end. As the parable of the vineyard (Mk 12:1–12) and other texts imply, this perspective served to indicate that Jesus' claims are not undermined by his crucifixion. Related in substance to this conception, but drawing on different Old Testament background, is a second approach that appeals to the psalms and the wisdom literature. Especially evident in the Passion narratives of the synoptic gospels, this perspective identified Jesus as the righteous sufferer, persecuted precisely because of his justice but eventually vindicated by God. While these two models could rest content with the insistence that Jesus' salvific significance is not destroyed by his shameful end, a third category of interpretation attributed redemptive, atoning value to the crucifixion itself. This theme, which makes considerable use of the Servant Songs of Isaiah 40–55, is reflected in the New Testament accounts of the Last Supper and in much Pauline material.

In addition to classifying early Christian interpretations of Jesus' death into these three basic categories, Schillebeeckx also maintains that some New Testament sources reflect the existence of early Christian communities that were not particularly troubled by Jesus' death and that therefore developed their christology with little or no attention to that subject. While this judgment, largely based on an argument from silence, is open to question, it is clear that the early church's reaction to the crucifixion was not uniform but included diverse strands of thought.

In addition to considering the treatment of Jesus' death in the formative years of Christianity, Schillebeeckx also examines in detail the thought of the New Testament authors themselves, with careful attention to their further development of the original themes. He remains convinced, however, that "New Testament Christianity can only be a model indirectly, and not directly" (*Christ*, p. 561) for later Christians. While committed to whatever is entailed by Jesus himself, Christians are free to articulate their faith in new and different ways; they are not bound to use categories standard in the past, even those deeply anchored in biblical tradition.

THE INTERPRETATION OF THE CRUCIFIXION IN SCHILLEBEECKX'S THEOLOGY

Unlike theologians who envision death as the final, climactic event of human freedom, Schillebeeckx stresses the passive character of death and its negative dimension. Such negativity is all the more evident in an unjust and violent execution like that of Jesus. God, the great opponent of human suffering, cannot have willed Jesus' passion and death in any direct sense. The immediate agents of the crucifixion were Jesus' enemies, who brutally removed him from our midst, and no theology can legitimately permit the memory of this evil to be blunted in subsequent glorification.

In keeping with these principles, Schillebeeckx insists that "first of all, we have to say that we are not redeemed *thanks to* the death of Jesus but *despite* it" (*Christ*, p. 729). Although he qualifies this comment by noting that the expression "despite the death" does not say enough, he judges that we lack categories suitable for filling this unfathomable "does not say enough" with meaningful content. While speaking at times of the value inherent in Jesus' death, Schillebeeckx's usual procedure is to locate salvific meaning elsewhere, either in Jesus' free acceptance of death (as distinct from death itself) or in divine conferral of value on Jesus' death through the resurrection.

Thus, on the whole, Schillebeeckx is more favorable to portrayals of the crucifixion as the death of a prophet-martyr and of the righteous sufferer than he is to interpretations of Jesus' death in the categories of atonement and redemption. The first two approaches, while largely bypassed in the history of theology, tend far more than the third to link Jesus' death to his public life, thus lending themselves to use in narrative presentations and thwarting impulses to isolate the crucifixion and interpret its meaning in purely theoretical fashion. Development of their content corresponds well to basic interests of Schillebeeckx's thought, especially since retrieval of neglected aspects of the Christian tradition is an important element in his overall theological program.

THE RESURRECTION

The resurrection inevitably poses problems for any effort to compose a narrative christology. Even the gospels do not attempt to provide a narrative of the resurrection itself, though they do of course affirm the resurrection in their stories about the finding of the empty tomb and the appearances of the risen Lord. Schillebeeckx's christology offers reflections on both the nature of the resurrection and the revelation of the risen Christ to his followers. To grasp accurately his position on these important issues, it is essential to remain alert to the distinction between the resurrection and its revelation.

THE NATURE OF THE RESURRECTION

Schillebeeckx's treatment of the resurrection is marked strongly by his insistence on the negative character of death. For this reason, he rules out any conception of the resurrection as "the other side of death"—a position common in the work of many modern theologians. Instead, Schillebeeckx sees Jesus' resurrection as a divine correcting victory over the negativity of his crucifixion, a new and different event after death that confers upon Jesus' death a new meaning. The resurrection is real and affects Jesus personally; without it, the historical Jesus would be merely a tragic failure. Nevertheless, the resurrection is meta-empirical and meta-historical—the ultimate reason why it cannot be narrated directly. For this reason too, the resurrection cannot be used appropriately as apologetic proof, since one statement of faith can never serve as legitimation for another.

THE REVELATION OF THE RISEN JESUS

Schillebeeckx's analyses of the revelation of the resurrection—one of the most controversial aspects of his theology—concentrate on New Testament traditions about the empty grave and the appearances, since gospel references to predictions of the resurrection by the historical Jesus are suspect of being products of the early church's christological reflection. Schillebeeckx's initial reconstruction has undergone some modification, largely in response to criticism of his work. Throughout, however, his position is characterized by the conviction—not shared by all theologians—that "there is not such a big difference between the way we are able, after Jesus' death, to come to faith in the crucified-and-risen One and the way in which the disciples of Jesus arrived at the same faith" (*Jesus*, p. 346).

In studying the empty grave stories, Schillebeeckx notes the discrepancies in the various accounts and concentrates on their function in the different gospels as articulations of the church's faith in Jesus' resurrection. Originally, he judged that the historical basis of these accounts can no longer be ascertained, since the tradition may originate from a later practice in Jerusalem of conducting Easter services at the site of Jesus' tomb. In response to widespread criticism of this hypothesis, Schillebeeckx now concludes that the grave may have been found empty, but still insists that this is not a factor in the public origin of Christian faith, for no visit to the tomb could as such provide sufficient basis for belief in Jesus' resurrection. Thus he, like most contemporary exegetes and theologians, concentrates chiefly on the New Testament tradition about appearances of the risen Jesus.

Schillebeeckx's analysis of the appearance tradition rests on his conviction that, since the disciples let Jesus down at the time of his arrest, some sort of conversion must lie between this failure and their later faith. In an unusual methodical procedure, he attempts to understand the gospel accounts of Jesus' appearances by examining the three New Testament narratives of Paul's experience on the road to Damascus (Acts 9; 22; 26). From a study of these texts, he concludes that the story of this event underwent gradual transformation from an account of Paul's conversion (Acts 9) through a transitional version (Acts 22) to a report of Paul's mission (Acts 26). The gospel narratives of Jesus' appearances to the disciples parallel the final form of the tradition about Paul, inasmuch as they too accent the theme of mission. In view of all these considerations, Schillebeeckx hypothesizes that the appearance narratives found in the gospels may be the end product of a tradition that in its early stages reflected the idea of conversion. He proposes that intimate personal religious experiences of a renewed divine offer of forgiveness of sin through Jesus led to the disciples reassembling at the initiative of Peter. This conversion experience is at the root of the ancient listing of appearances in 1 Corinthians 15:3–8. The later gospel appearance narratives are not historical reports, but theological elaborations of specific aspects of the church's faith in Jesus' resurrection.

Schillebeeckx's initial writing on the appearance tradition, like his study of the empty grave, has been subjected to considerable criticism, and he has modified his position in response to some objections. His later treatments of the issue refrain from stressing the theme of conversion experiences and consider the historical genesis of belief in the resurrection an open question, provided only that its divine source is recognized and that supranaturalistic conceptions of the origin and growth of the disciples' faith are excluded.

In any case, the story of Jesus does not end with resurrection appearances. In addition to weighing those features of Jesus that constituted an offer of salvation from God, christology must also attend to Christians' expression of what they have experienced in encounter with Jesus and how they have responded to him in faith. In considering this material, it will be well to bear in mind Schillebeeckx's insistence that "there is no gap between Jesus' self-understanding and the Christ proclaimed by the Church" (*Jesus*, p. 312).

EARLY CHRISTIAN INTERPRETATIONS OF JESUS

In examining the history of Christian thought about Jesus, Schillebeeckx is especially attentive to the seminal period (roughly two decades) between Jesus' death and the writing of Paul's Epistles, the oldest books of the New Testament. In view of the limitations of the available sources, we can only seek to reconstruct the thought of this first Christian generation by extrapolating from the traces preserved in later texts. While acknowledging the inevitably tentative nature of such research, Schillebeeckx adapts some analyses of Helmut Koester to offer a plausible summary of the diverse assessments Jesus evoked from the earliest Christians.

Following Koester, Schillebeeckx distinguishes four distinct creedal tendencies present in early Christianity. A "parousia christology" concentrated on Jesus' future role as son of man and coming judge, while a second type, sometimes termed a "divine man christology," presented Jesus chiefly as a worker of miracles. "Wisdom christology" remembered Jesus as teacher and collected his sayings; in some subspecies, it identified Jesus as wisdom incarnate. (The christological doctrine of the early ecumenical councils is a further development of this model, which has thus proven quite influential on Christian thinking.) Lastly, an "Easter christology," reflected strongly in the Pauline writings, directed attention toward Jesus' death and resurrection. Each of these trajectories of early Christian thought captured a real facet of Jesus' life and for that reason should be recognized as fundamentally legitimate.

Nonetheless, none of the four early strands of interpretation of Jesus was fully comprehensive, and none, in Schillebeeckx' judgment, is able in itself to account for the merger of the four trajectories in the canonical books of the New Testament. For this reason, diverging from Koester, Schillebeeckx posits the existence of a more basic category, one that preceded the differentiation of the four trajectories and laid the foundation for their later unification. Sifting through the evidence in the New Testament, he weighs three models available in the Jewish tradition of the day that could have been adopted for this purpose: eschatological prophet, messianic son of David, and son of man. While all three of these titles were eventually applied to Jesus, Schillebeeckx judges that eschatological prophet was the original basic category. Son of man suggested an otherworldly figure, and messiah required extensive reinterpretation to avoid inappropriate nationalistic connotations. Eschatological prophet—the long-awaited prophet like Moses (cf. Dt 18:15–18) who speaks with God face to face and bears God's final word—was suitable for conveying Jesus' location in the prophetic tradition and his superiority over all other prophets. Rich in theological implications, this initial identification of Jesus captured well the facts of his life; in due course, it also gave rise to the other titles and the later christological trajectories.

Schillebeeckx's treatment of later New Testament elaborations of its basic theme of definitive salvation from God in Jesus will be considered in the following chapter on his soteriology and theology of grace. Their value and the value of postbiblical products of further Christological reflection are largely to be measured by how adequately they reflect a full and comprehensive picture of Jesus. For the final norm and criterion of any interpretation of Jesus of Nazareth is Jesus of Nazareth himself.

, CONCLUSION

To a greater extent than any other contemporary systematic theologian, Edward Schillebeeckx has developed his christological position in detailed confrontation with the texts of the New Testament and with the issues raised and examined in modern biblical scholarship. His work also reflects keen awareness of recent philosophical currents and of the twentieth-century problems Christian faith is required to address. For these reasons, his writings on christology offer instructive access to the current state of research regarding Jesus; they are especially valuable for indicating concretely where the chief disputed questions lie. At the same time, they provide a rich resource for deepened personal reflection on Jesus of Nazareth as foundation and object of

Christian faith. Here Schillebeeckx's insistence on the insepara-bility of Jesus' message from his person and on the interconnec-tion of Jesus' public life and death are particularly important.

Nevertheless, as is only to be expected in a project of this scope, serious questions may still be raised about various aspects of Schil-lebeeckx's thought. Is he correct in his emphasis on the category of the eschatological prophet for understanding the historical Je-sus and reconstructing the development of christology in the ear-ly church? Does his assessment of the crucifixion in primarily negative terms do full justice to the importance of Jesus' death and to the fact that Jesus' manner of life brought him to this end? Does his treatment of the resurrection as a divine correcting tri-umph over death's negativity unintentionally devalue the signifi-cance of this life? Is his reconstruction of the origin of Christian faith in Jesus' resurrection historically plausible and convincing? More generally, does his preference for narrative over theory im-ply some false dilemmas, and does his concentration on the prob-lem of evil impede access to certain other dimensions of a full presentation of Jesus?

Whatever the answers to these questions may be, Schille-beeckx's narrative Christology remains a major contribution to contemporary theology and a rewarding source for modern Christians to use in their efforts to reflect anew on the central ob-ject of their faith.

SUGGESTIONS FOR FURTHER READING

The chief sources for Schillebeeckx's Christology are of course his massive *Jesus: An Experiment in Christology* and *Christ: The Expe-rience of Jesus as Lord*. Schillebeeckx has responded to various crit-ics of these works in his *Interim Report on the Books "Jesus" and "Christ"*. In addition, documentation of his extensive correspon-dence and conversation with the Congregation for the Doctrine of the Faith with regard to his christology has been published in *The Schillebeeckx Case*. These later works have helped clarify some aspects of his thought.

Yet these volumes, however important, are not fully suitable for readers seeking an introduction to Schillebeeckx's christology. Some shorter texts are of more value for this purpose. While *The*

Church with a Human Face is chiefly concerned with issues concerning ministry, the christological section of its opening chapter (pp. 13–34) offers a succinct and readily accessible summary of Schillebeeckx's thought on Jesus. *On Christian Faith* (pp. 15–30) contains a similar condensation. Finally, three chapters (pp. 33–44, 103–15, 180–87) in *God Among Us*, a collection of Schillebeeckx's sermons, lectures, and essays on spiritual topics are equally useful in this regard. Taken together, "Jesus the Prophet," "I Believe in the Man Jesus: The Christ, the Only Beloved Son, Our Lord," and "How Shall We Sing the Lord's Song in a Strange Land? (Ps. 137:4)" provide a reliable guide to Schillebeeckx's chief christological themes, as his positions on the nature of soteriology, the necessity of narrative theology, the identification of Jesus as eschatological prophet, the theological significance of Jesus' public life, and the principles needed to interpret the crucifixion and understand the resurrection are all clearly articulated. These shorter pieces are recommended as the best avenues of approach to Schillebeeckx's retelling of the story of Jesus as a story of God.

5. Salvation from God in Jesus the Christ: Soteriology

JANET M. CALLEWAERT

For nearly two thousand years Christianity has made the extraordinary claim that Jesus Christ is the salvation of the world. In spite of this "good news" sin, misery, and oppression have continued to plague human existence. This paradox has been heightened by the concrete realities of the nuclear age. Today two-thirds of the world's population are exploited and oppressed by the remaining third, which is composed of opposing power blocs in the East and West. All attempts to resolve this conflict appear to be impeded by mutual suspicion, mistrust, and blame. The world seems to be on the brink of destruction. The acuteness of this situation presses the question whether Jesus can still be experienced as salvation today. What bearing does Christian faith in Jesus as God's salvation have on the realities of the contemporary world?

It was with the intention of addressing these questions that Edward Schillebeeckx initiated a process of investigation and critical reflection that has resulted in the monumental works *Jesus* and *Christ*. While awaiting the third volume in the projected three-part series, the structure of the project to date consists of three distinct but interrelated movements: the christology of *Jesus*, an analysis of New Testament understandings of salvation, and a first move toward a contemporary soteriology. This investigation is motivated by the hope of providing a new focus for traditional Western christology, a perspective Schillebeeckx feels is much needed in light of the critical question whether it is still possible to experience Christian salvation. He sees the challenge to be that of creating new traditions in and through which the good news of God's salvation in Jesus becomes activated and actualized in today's world.

In his christology Schillebeeckx seeks to discover in the image of Jesus reconstructed by historical criticism what is unique and particular about Jesus of Nazareth that led from pre-Easter discipleship to the New Testament confession of Jesus as definitive salvation from God. Schillebeeckx contends that only after a critically reconstructed picture of Jesus' message, way of life, and consequent execution has been obtained is it possible to discover how the whole of this could have been experienced as "salvation" at that time. In a further step it can be asked how people today might experience the "final good" in this Jesus event.

In the introduction to *Christ* Schillebeeckx clarifies the immediate connection between the first two moments of his emerging soteriology. Whereas in *Jesus* Schillebeeckx's concern is with those aspects of the "historical Jesus" that may have led to the New Testament confession of him, in *Christ* his attention shifts to the New Testament elaboration of the ongoing experience of Jesus as salvation from God. In other words, the focus of *Christ* is the continuation of the process of identifying Jesus of Nazareth that began with an initial encounter between Jesus and some first-century Jews who "followed after" him during his ministry and then later knew him to be alive and present beyond death in the community of believers. Through this encounter with Jesus the first community of disciples found renewed meaning and purpose in their lives.

The experience of renewed life in Jesus, the crucified-and-risen One, led the disciples to further reflection. They began to analyze their experience and to consider its various aspects in terms of available socioreligious models. Familiar things were viewed from a new focal point. "On the basis of their common experience they arrived at what we might call a Christian theory of grace, the beginnings of what in Christian tradition is called a 'theology of grace': soteriology, a thematic account of the meaning of Christian redemption and Christian salvation" (*Christ*, pp. 19–20). The experience of salvation from God in and through Jesus found written expression in the corpus of writings that form the New Testament. In these documents the meaning of grace points to a Christian oneness of experience that found great variety in expression according to the historical socioreligious circumstances of the New Testament communities.

Schillebeeckx understands this basic experience to be the constant unitive factor of Christian faith. By "oneness of experience" he means a communal-ecclesial experience "which obliges people to define the ultimate meaning and purport of their lives by reference to Jesus of Nazareth." In more traditional terms this means a common experience "which causes people to interpret Jesus life as the definitive or eschatological activity of God in history for the salvation or deliverance of men and women. The constant unitive factor . . . is that particular groups of people find final salvation imparted by God in Jesus of Nazareth" (*Jesus*, p. 56; cf. *Christ*, p. 463).

In Part II of *Christ* Schillebeeckx explores the question of how the New Testament communities expressed the one basic experience of salvation from God in Jesus according to the horizons of their concrete historical experiences and understandings. The purpose of this inquiry is to discover a normative orientation and inspiration for a contemporary soteriology. In Part III Schillebeeckx concludes his investigation with a synthetic description of the four structural elements he contends must be present in any contemporary theology of grace that is both faithful to the gospel and relevant to the present.

NEW TESTAMENT UNDERSTANDINGS OF GRACE

From his analysis of New Testament scholarship Schillebeeckx derives a descriptive theological synthesis in which grace emerges as a new way of life given by God in Jesus the Christ. In the New Testament grace means the sovereignly free, unconditional love of God manifested in history as a merciful and compassionate concern for human beings, especially for those who experience the greatest need. It is asserted throughout the New Testament that the historical appearing of Jesus is the grace of God. Although the entire earthly life of Jesus is the proffer of God's salvation, Jesus' self-giving to the point of death—that is, his suffering and death on the cross—is the all-embracing sign of grace in the New Testament. Without the resurrection, however, the earthly life and dying of Jesus remain open and problematic. Thus in the New Testament "the death and resurrection of Jesus are the determinative climax of the grace of God in Jesus the Christ"

(*Christ*, p. 467). Only then does Jesus become the source of God's saving grace. Only the risen Jesus imparts eschatological salvation, that is, the gift of the Spirit.

In the resurrection Jesus acquires a community whereby the good news of God's salvation in Jesus continues to be proclaimed in human history. By grace the Christian is given a new identity in Christ that is a new mode of existence. As existence in grace, Christian life is patterned after God's unconditional love as manifested in Jesus' person, message, and praxis of the kingdom even unto death. This way of life is a new alternative for human living that is made possible through a share in the relationship that binds Jesus to the Father through the Spirit. Thus the New Testament understanding of grace has both a mystical and an ethical dimension.

As a way of life Christian existence in grace is given concrete form in specific sociohistorical circumstances. Schillebeeckx sees the New Testament churches as graced communities sent forth as a critical and creative consciousness to actualize the righteousness of God in human history. In this way the New Testament indirectly provides a model for "the building up of Christian communities in the world and for the forming of a better society" (*Christ*, p. 560). The particular form that grace takes is something that must be continually decided anew according to the sociocultural conditions of historical existence. Therefore, it is necessary to complement a theological analysis of grace with an analysis of historical circumstances.

On the basis of his investigation of New Testament understandings of grace Schillebeeckx makes several observations he judges as pertinent to a contemporary appropriation of the Christian experience of salvation. First, a given tradition of grace undergoes continual development and reinterpretation as it is lived out historically. Second, since it is historically situated, an experience of grace takes place within already existing sociocultural and religious patterns of experience and interpretation. While being sympathetic to these patterns of interpretation, Christianity must maintain a critical function in regard to the structures and models that it assimilates into its experience. Third, the New Testament theology of grace is comprised of distinct, alternative, and complementary traditions, namely, the synoptic, Pauline, and Johannine traditions. From this fact Schillebeeckx concludes that in new historical situations it is not only permissible but necessary to develop new traditions that are faithful to the one basic experience of salvation from God in Jesus. Thus "every community throughout the world has to write its own history of the living Jesus. . . . The account of the life of Christians in the world in which they live is a fifth gospel; it also belongs at the heart of Christology" (*Christ*, pp. 18, 425).

Before taking up the question of a contemporary experience of Christian salvation Schillebeeckx proposes four structural elements that must be taken into account in any current soteriology that is both rooted in the apostolic tradition and relevant to the present historical situation. First, God and the divine history with human beings: God has self-revealed as a sovereignly free God of unconditional love whose "cause" is the furthering of human well-being and happiness. "As Creator, God is the author of good and the antagonist of evil, . . . the guarantor that human life has a positive and significant meaning" (*Christ*, p. 638). God's glory lies in the happiness and salvation of humankind. Second, the nucleus of God's history with human beings is found in Jesus the Christ. The person of Jesus in his life and above all in his death in unbroken communion with God reveals the meaning and purpose of human existence, which has its source and fulfillment in the God of Jesus who is unconditional love. Third, human history as discipleship: as the bond between Jesus and Christian communities, the gift of the Spirit is both a share in Jesus' relationship with God and a mandate to continue the history of Jesus in the world. "Therefore we can only speak of the history of Jesus in terms of the story of the Christian community which follows Jesus" (*Christ*, p. 642). Fourth, the eschatological consummation of human history: definitive salvation belongs to the absolute freedom of God who will bring the good begun in human history to its final consummation in a way that transcends all expectations. The way that the New Testament gives specific form to these four dimensions of the experience of grace provides a normative orientation for future generations of Christians. In fidelity to the apostolic tradition the present generation must articulate its own theology of grace.

THE PRESENT SITUATION

What became an ethical imperative for Christians of the New Testament period was the result of their historical situation. The demands and responsibilities that confronted the first generations of Christians were on a different level than those faced by Christians today. Hence, a conscious fidelity to the apostolic norm of the gospel necessitates a critical understanding of the urgent demands and responsibilities of people today to whom the same good news is directed.

Ethics was separated from religion as a result of the process of secularization that began in the Enlightenment. The danger of detaching the human person from ethics is a further consequence of the emancipation of ethics from theology. This threat is being experienced today in the demand for a value-free ethics that rejects not only religion but also modern secularized ethics based on a human foundation. As Schillebeeckx observes, value-free ethics are "setting *our very humanity* at risk" (*Christ*, p. 658).

In Schillebeeckx's assessment the situation of estrangement between ethics and religion means that Christianity must accord ethics a certain priority over religion. This is not to deny the reciprocal relationship between ethics and religion. Ethics is essentially concerned with the basic questions: what the human being is; how, therefore, human beings should live; and for what kind of humanity must we finally decide. These basic ethical questions are intrinsically connected with worldviews and religious options. In other words, the question of the final significance of human existence is implied in every question of ethical immediacy.

The concrete historical reality, however, is humankind in need. The fact is that the vast majority of the world's population suffers at the hands of the privileged few. The suffering masses do not suffer "on account of righteousness"; they do not suffer for the "sake of the kingdom," for a good cause. They suffer "exploitation, oppression or rejection not only from individual human beings but above all from socio-political, economic and bureaucratic systems, anonymous forces which are nonetheless real" (*Christ*, p. 650). Because of the urgency of this situation people cannot wait for a unanimous view of the final significance of human life. *This* human being must be given direct and effective help both interpersonally and through social structures. Thus the specific historical starting point for any ethics is the threatened *humanum*. The ethical imperative is not an abstract norm but "an event *which presents a challenge:* our concrete history itself" (*Christ*, p. 659). In specific terms this means that the "ethically good" is that which realizes the good and overcomes evil in respect of the actual situation. In other words, ethics is concerned with a praxis of liberation and reconciliation.

Furthermore, because of the vast expansion of scientific technology the consequences of human activity no longer simply pertain to individuals and small groups. "Regardless of their specific group or their cultural and ethical traditions, all nations and cultures are confronted by our present civilization with a general ethical problem which applies to them all" (*Christ*, p. 660). What is at stake is the future of humankind. On a global level humankind is faced with the critical charge of deciding the future of the world, the future of humanity, and humanity's meaning. What is needed is an ethics of worldwide responsibility that can guarantee not only human survival but also meaningful human survival. This challenge, however, poses the further question of what is a meaningful humanity. Is there a universally valid view on this question?

The human person is a "being caught up in history." Human "*nature* is itself a history, a historical event, and is not simply *given*" (*Christ*, p. 732). In other words, humanity is a future reality that can only be achieved in the course of human history. The dilemma of human history as a history of suffering makes the task of realizing the *humanum* both pressing and perplexing. In matter of fact, the question of how to achieve a livable humanity comes from concrete conditions of alienation and human woundedness of various kinds. "Salvation and humanity being saved, integrity in a truly human and free way is in fact the *theme* of the whole of human history" (*Christ*, p. 732). Thus human beings have become conscious of the fact that human history is the place where salvation or human wholeness is decided on; and the decision is an explicitly conscious one.

Given that the *humanum* is a future reality, Schillebeeckx contends that in directing the task of achieving a livable humanity human beings have at their disposal no more than a set of anthropological constants. These constants present constitutive conditions that must always be presupposed in any human action if humanity is to be livable. Schillebeeckx identifies seven such constants, which he sees "as a kind of system of co-ordinates, the focal point of which is personal identity within social culture" (*Christ*, p. 733). In delineating these constitutive aspects of humanity, his expressed concern is "the creative establishment of specific norms for a better assessment of human worth and thus for human *salvation*" (*Christ*, p. 734).

The first anthropological constant is the relationship of human beings to their corporeality and via this corporeality to nature and the ecological environment. A balance must be maintained between the value of technology and that of aesthetic and enjoyable converse with nature. The second constant is the human being's essential relatedness to others. The structure of personal identity includes the element of being together through which one shares oneself with others and is confirmed in existence and personhood.

The third essential dimension of humanity is the relationship of the person to social and institutional structures. As a dimension of personal identity, social structures deeply influence human inwardness and personhood. Although structures and institutions develop into an objective form of society, they do not exist independently of human reason and the human will to preserve them. There exists an ethical demand to change such structures and institutions when they enslave and debase human beings rather than liberate and protect them.

Schillebeeckx identifies the fourth anthropological constant as the conditioning of people by time and space. The abiding dialectical tension between nature and history means that there are forms of suffering and threats to human life and well-being that cannot be removed by technology and social intervention. Because of its historicity, human existence is a task of understanding one's own situation and unmasking critically the meaninglessness that human beings bring about in their history. This means "that the presumption of adopting a standpoint outside *historical* action and thought is a danger to true humanity" (*Christ*, p. 739).

The fifth anthropological constant is the essential relationship between theory and practice. As a historical process of changing meanings, human culture needs permanence. A mutual relationship of theory and practice is the only humanly responsible guarantee of a permanent culture that is increasingly worthy of the *humanum*.

The sixth dimension of humanity is the religious and "parareligious" consciousness of the human being. This constant finds expression in a variety of different utopian conceptions of life that seek to give meaning and context to human existence in the world. In most utopias the human person is understood as the active subject of history without being the all-controlling principle that is responsible for the whole of history and its final outcome. This principle is called fate by some, evolution by others, and humankind by yet others. For the religious person this is the living God. A utopian view "is always a *form of faith,* in the sense of a 'utopia' which cannot be scientifically demonstrated, or at least can never be completely rationalized" (*Christ,* p. 741). Schillebeeckx asserts that in this way "faith" is an anthropological constant throughout human history, a constant without which humane and livable human life and action become impossible.

Because human culture is an irreducible synthesis of the six anthropological constants, the synthesis itself is a constant. This synthesis constitutes the reality that heals human beings and brings them salvation. The six constants mutually influence one another. They delineate the basic form of human existence and hold one another in balance. Undervaluation of one of these dimensions threatens the whole, thereby damaging human society and culture.

The anthropological constants, however, do no more than present constitutive conditions for a livable humanity. Specific norms must be worked out on the basis of these values. The task of creating such norms is an imperative that confronts human beings here and now. Moreover, there will always be pluralism in the area of specific norms even though the same basic values are recognized. Learning to live with pluralism is one of the tasks of a livable modern humanity. Nevertheless, if ethical norms are to be viable they must be capable of being tested in valid intersubjective discussion. This holds even if the basic inspiration comes from a religious belief.

CHRISTIAN SALVATION

The problem of the relationship between the ethics of human liberation and the grace of redemption is of central concern for a contemporary mediation of Christian salvation. There is ample evidence that a widespread pluralism exists in respect to this question. The relevance of the Christian gospel for a social and political world order is neither clear nor self-evident. In a first move towards offering a solution to the problem Schillebeeckx affirms the dialectical relationship between interior and social freedom as well as between religious traditions and the sociohistorical circumstances in which they originate and develop.

True liberation or salvation is overcoming all personal and social forms of alienation. It is the "being-in-wholeness" of the human person and history. If people are to grasp what Christians mean by salvation they must have some experience of human liberation. Schillebeeckx therefore raises the question "whether the freedom of the children of God is not pointed towards a social liberation as an integral ingredient of eschatological salvation from God. In other words, the question whether Christian freedom or redemption is not directed towards political and social liberation as a condition of its own possibility" (*Christ*, p. 745).

It is characteristic of the structure of the development of Christian faith that Christians uncover latent dimensions in their tradition as a result of stimuli introduced by the sociocultural circumstances in which the tradition is historically situated. Although the gospel of Jesus is an inclusive message of freedom and love for all people, the consequences of this "good news" are only gradually revealed in the ongoing development of human consciousness. It is quite possible, then, that at a particular historical moment an emancipatory process of liberation can become a necessary demand of historically situated Christian love. Nevertheless, because it is precisely in their service to God that religions are also a service to human beings and the world, it is necessary that Christians investigate the particular religious and critical force of their solidarity with emancipation movements. At issue here is whether believers and nonbelievers simply do the same thing under different names or whether the Christian gospel gives a service to the world which is specifically religious.

Whereas religion must draw on an experience of God in order to be of service to the world, Western scientific technology has created sociocultural conditions in which the possibility of experiencing God is no longer simply taken for granted. A highly scientific and technological experience of the world in Western societies has made faith more difficult than in the past. The crucial question is whether it is possible for the contemporary Western person to have a direct relationship with God.

Schillebeeckx posits the experience of creatureliness as the foundation of all religious awareness. By this he means "an experience of ourselves, others and the world in which we feel as a norm something which transcends at least our arbitrary control of ourselves" (*Christ*, p. 811). It is an experience of givenness which is the root of all religion as a mediated immediate relationship with God. "Mediated immediacy" concerns the unique relationship between finite beings and the infinite God who is absolute origin. Whereas the term "immediate" refers to the divine manner of the real presence of the creator to the creature, "mediate" describes the mode in which people encounter the divine presence. God is directly and creatively present in the creature. In this case mediation does not destroy immediacy but produces it. All that is not God derives the totality of its existence and activity from the creator who as absolute freedom transcends all things through interiority. This means that the living God is the depth dimension of all reality. The fundamental medium of the creator is creation. The relationship between the infinite creator and the finite creature is mediated through an encounter with the world, human history, and human beings.

The structure of the presence of God as mediated immediacy implies that the human response to God has a similar structure of mediation. In other words, although religion cannot be reduced to cohumanity and sociopolitical concerns, it cannot do without this mediation. God's grace is present *in* the structure of historical human experience and praxis; it is the whole of reality in which human beings live and of which they are a part. Because of the constitutive relationship between personal identity and the social structures that provide freedom, sociopolitical improvements form an integral part of what is experienced as the grace of God. In the same way it is possible to experience God's saving nearness in both the humane and natural sciences. These are the contemporary realities in and through which God is experienced in terms of Western culture. "Here the divine reality proves itself to be a *reality,* as the one who wills good and opposes evil, the liberator from alienation" (*Christ,* p. 814). It follows that wherever human liberation is possible, it remains a universal human task in the name of God. Wherever good is promoted and evil is resisted God's saving grace is being realized in and through a human praxis. There is no dichotomy between what is done by God and what is done by human beings who have their foundation in God.

The liberation of Christian freedom, however, is not identical with programs and processes of human emancipation. Alienation in human life can never be entirely overcome. There is a human suffering that persists even in optimal social structures; to a great extent nature remains alien to human beings; and then there is also the reality of human finitude, a source of anxiety as well as trust in God. Human impotence becomes particularly evident in the consciousness of human sinfulness. A final healing of the division in human existence in the world can only be the consequence of an absolute freedom and creative love that embraces the whole of reality.

Consequently, all hope for the future based on human creativity must be taken up into a hope founded on God's own saving creativity. For this reason all human self-liberation stands under the divine proviso. A critical religious consciousness recognizes the manifestation of God's saving nearness in any action that promotes human well-being while at the same time it opposes a complete identification of human salvation with any given or anticipated sociopolitical form. The history of redemption can neither be identified with nor detached from the history of emancipation. Christian salvation is an historical mediation of God's saving immediacy. In other words, it includes both mystical-contemplative and sociopolitical dimensions.

Schillebeeckx calls the fundamental awareness of God's mediated-but-nevertheless-real immediacy the mystical aspect of belief in God. This mystical depth in which the immediacy of God is the essential element can be experienced in both positive and negative ways. There are positive disclosure experiences of the givenness and goodness of life in which there occurs a change in perception from the mediating to the mediated, that is, God's presence. Schillebeeckx understands "explicit prayer" as a person's effort to see this immediacy. Immediacy can also be experienced as a "dark night," that is, as "a nothingness of fullness": God's presence as a pure experience of faith communicated in the mediation of extreme negativity. Faith is certainly more than a theoretical conviction when it persists even when "every empirical foundation and every guarantee have been removed and one weeps over the fiasco of one's life" (*Christ*, p. 815).

The mediation of God's presence in negative experience is particularly relevant to contemporary circumstances. In spite of tremendous advances in human civilization that have been brought about by scientific technology, human freedom is plagued with a sense of anxiety about the present and the future. All is not progress: human beings have created and perpetuated a history that is dark with suffering and oppression. To believe in God is to entrust oneself, others and the whole of history to the unnameable God whose identity can only be guessed at in an historical process: hidden humanity in search of the hidden God. The reality of the history of human suffering continues in spite of the progress of human emancipation and in spite of God's redemptive action in Jesus. The fact that both redemption and emancipation are found within conditions of suffering gives an inner tension to any understanding of redemption and any attempt at self-liberation.

Human suffering, however, also has a productive and critical epistemological value. As an experience of contrast, suffering includes characteristics of both contemplative and practical forms of knowledge. On the one hand, although in the form of negative experience, suffering comes upon one in a way that is similar to the passive structure of positive contemplative experiences. On the other hand, under the aspect of critical negativity the experience of suffering resists the passivity of the contemplative dimension in a way that leads to a possible action that will overcome both suffering and its causes. As an experience of contrast suffering indirectly implies an awareness of the possible positive significance of the *humanum*. It follows that action to overcome suffering is possible only through an implicit anticipation of a potential universal significance to come. Thus the particular productive and critical epistemological value of the experience of contrast in suffering is a knowledge that looks for and opens up the future. Schillebeeckx concludes that in the present historical circumstances contemplation and action can only be connected through the criticism of the history of suffering and the ethical awareness that comes to birth in it.

The particular history of Jesus of Nazareth is part of the history of accumulated human suffering. Jesus' message of the unconditional love of God and corresponding praxis of solidarity with socioreligious outcasts met with violent opposition and rejection. In the cross of Jesus the religious implication of this rejection is made manifest. The notion of God's saving immediacy in the mediation of extreme negativity is central to Schillebeeckx's understanding of the saving significance of the death of Jesus. His position is that it is precisely as an historical failure surmounted by the absolute freedom of God that Jesus' death is saving in history. The redemptive force of this death does not lie with suffering and the negativity of failure as such but with unbroken religious communion and solidarity to the point of death. In the radical alienation of suffering and death Jesus lives out the meaning of God's rule as sovereignly free but total solidarity with people. Because Jesus persevered in trust and communion with God even to his death on the cross, the failure of the cross is reevaluated. Jesus was successful by virtue of his unbroken communion with God. Death is defeated and new life is opened up on the other side of death: "life's relatedness to God cannot be impaired by suffering and death for anyone who, like Jesus, goes on trusting in God" (*Jesus*, pp. 648–649). Christian faith in the resurrection does not explain death. Rather, it proclaims the "good news" that death is not accorded the last word which belongs to the "nevertheless" of God's future.

As the correction of the negativity of death, Schillebeeckx understands the resurrection as an event that is both new and different from Jesus' suffering and death. Yet this does not mean that he views the resurrection as an extrinsic addition. He cautions against seeing the death of Jesus as a failure in the dimension of human history that on a suprahistorical, transcendent level is transformed by God into a divine victory while leaving the historical experience a human failure. God's transcendent triumph over human failure is incorporated into Jesus' enduring love for

God and human beings *during* and *in* the historical moment of his failure on the cross. The surmounting of death in the resurrection is God's definitive acceptance and final fulfillment of the earthly life of Jesus. It is precisely in this way that the cross of Jesus acquires a productive and critical force in the dimension of human history.

In spite of the disruption caused by the fatal rejection of Jesus' person and message there is continuity between the hidden dimension of what took place on the cross and its manifestation in the resurrection. In the death and resurrection of Jesus the human rejection of God's offer of salvation and the persistence of this offer extended in the risen Jesus meet each other. "Through the resurrection God actually breaks that rejection of definitive salvation." (*Jesus*, p. 641.) God's living presence is an "undeserved abundance" of meaning stronger and more penetrating than the abundance of non-meaning that is the ultimate enemy, death. Schillebeeckx describes God's triumph over death as the "eternally new event" of God's divinity which brings earthly life to fulfillment. It is the "end-grace": the gracious gift of God's redemption to the whole person. Whereas death is a radical no to human history, the resurrection is a definitive yes to this history whereby earthly history is perpetuated for eternity as God's history.

The living God who is the future of human history is in the risen Jesus the presence of the future. In this way Christian faith finds in Jesus the promise and the possibility that human history can be realized as a history of salvation. Jesus is the ultimate meaning of human history. At the same time, however, the Christian confession of Jesus as the savior of the world is a claim to universality without exclusivity. Jesus lived and died out of the radical conviction of God's universal love and compassion and, therefore, opposed adamantly any separatist, sectarian view that would restrict the freedom of the living God of salvation to a "holy few." For Schillebeeckx Jesus has universal significance precisely because he reveals the true identity of the one God and in and through that the disclosure of true humanity. Jesus' *Abba* is "the (monotheistic) God of Jews, Muslims, Christians, and so many others . . . the One who liberates and yet at the same time—however incomprehensibly—is the final arbiter of meaning, the 'Creator of heaven and earth' " (*Jesus*, p. 31.) Through Jesus' historical self-giving unto death, God self-reveals as the God whose innermost being is the salvation of human beings. In spite of all empirical evidence to the contrary, God's cause is the human cause and God can be trusted to bring the whole of creation to completion. This is the "good news" that the Christian gospel offers the world. As such it is a renewing power and a subversive force in history that refuses to give death and destruction the last word.

Christian faith in the resurrection is already a victory over death that radicalizes present earthly life in that it liberates believers from self-concern and frees them for an unconditional dedication to the bettering of human existence in history. Given the fact that the history of suffering and oppression continues, a hope supported by faith in the resurrection will always lead to a praxis of resisting evil and furthering good. Indeed, believing in a universal meaning of history only validates itself in a course of action that tries to overcome human suffering in the strength of the religious conviction that things can be otherwise. In other words, the Christian message will be critically productive, credible, and capable of offering hope to the world only if it is a consistent praxis which gives concrete form to a living communion with God in Jesus the Christ.

Definitive salvation transcends present experience. Although everything is decided in human history, the last word is not with history but with the living God whose absolute presence supports finitude. The possible despair that can be caused by the contingency and woundedness of human existence is taken up and transcended by the inexhaustible abundance of God. Divine possibilities cannot be limited to earthly expectations and achievements. Nevertheless, partial salvation is realized whenever and wherever human existence is confirmed and furthered. In this way human love—supported by absolute love—becomes the sacrament and promise of God's redemptive love offered to the whole of humanity. Thus in spite of the ongoing history of human suffering there are already fragments of eschatological joy in human history. Moreover, it is only on the basis of partial experiences of salvation that the Christian message and promise of definitive salvation in Jesus the Christ can take on real meaning and provide a stimulus for eschatological hope.

The fragmentary and partial character of all experiences of redemption and liberation makes it impossible to reconcile theoretically the redemption already accomplished with the concrete history of human suffering. The practical Christian alternative to this theoretical impotence is the eschatological remembrance of Jesus the Christ. Schillebeeckx locates the particular character of Christian *anamnesis* in the biblical notion that God remembers the divine saving deeds of the past through new saving acts in the present. This means that the particular critical and productive force of the *memoria passionis Christi* is communicated by the living Christian community in so far as it is an active *memoria passionis* of the risen Lord. The church is a living *memoria Christi* to the extent that its praxis makes Jesus' service of reconciliation visibly present as promise and historical ferment. There is a real possibility for an experience of God in a way of life which is patterned after Jesus' life of unconditional dedication to God and service of others. Although complete redemption is not within human power, God "*gives a future* to all our action towards liberation and reconciliation, a future which is greater than the volume of finite history" (*Christ*, p. 838).

SUGGESTIONS FOR FURTHER READING

Schillebeeckx's investigation of the New Testament theology of the experience of grace is found in Part Two of *Christ*. This lengthy study is followed in Part Three by a concluding synthesis in which Schillebeeckx proposes four structural elements that he sees as indispensable for a contemporary theology of grace. Pertinent passages from this material are found in Part Four of *The Schillebeeckx Reader.*

While Schillebeeckx directly addresses the question of a contemporary soteriology in Part Four of *Christ*, he anticipates issues pertinent to this undertaking in Part Four of *Jesus*. Significant selections from *Jesus*, *Christ* and *Interim Report* are found in Part Three of *The Schillebeeckx Reader*. A number of homilies in *God Among Us* highlight aspects of Schillebeeckx's developing soteriology. See in particular, "I Believe in Eternal Life", "Belief in 'a New Heaven and a New Earth' " and "Belief in Jesus as Salvation for the Outcast". God's salvation in Jesus is discussed in connection with creation and the biblical notion of the kingdom in "Kingdom of God: Creation and Salvation" in *Interim Report*. Cf. "I Believe in God, Creator of Heaven and Earth" and "I Believe in the Man Jesus: the Christ, the Only Beloved Son, Our Lord" in *God Among Us*. That a contemporary praxis of saving grace continues to be of urgent concern for Schillebeeckx is evident in *On Christian Faith*. See especially, "Who or What Brings Salvation to Men and Women? The World and God" and "Jesus as the Question of Men and Women to God: Mysticism, Ethics and Politics".

6. Presence to God, Presence to the World: Spirituality

DONALD J. GOERGEN, O.P.

For Edward Schillebeeckx, spirituality is not just one aspect of human life that can be singled out for particular attention. Rather, for Christians, spirituality is the whole of human life interpreted from the perspective of authentic Christian praxis. Although all of Schillebeeckx's works can be construed as a theology of Christian praxis, some of them focus more specifically on Christian praxis or on the conventional theme of the spiritual life.

Schillebeeckx himself has been influenced by the Dominican tradition in spirituality, of which he himself is both an exponent and also "a new moment." He has written on Dominic, Albert the Great, Thomas Aquinas, and others. He has acknowledged the influence of modern Dominicans, particularly Marie-Dominique Chenu, who probably more than anyone else was Schillebeeckx's inspiration. Chenu guided Schillebeeckx's early doctoral dissertation on the sacraments, and it was Chenu who introduced the phrase "signs of the times" into modern Catholic theology. If one wanted to trace the development of modern Catholic thought and spirituality from Chenu through the present writings of Schillebeeckx, one might entitle it, "From the 'Signs of the Times' to 'Political Holiness.' "

Underlying this development and a key to understanding Schillebeeckx is the foundational idea of *présence au monde.* The term originated with the Dominican Henri Lacordaire. It was developed by Chenu, had its influence at the Second Vatican Council, and has been consciously acknowledged by Schillebeeckx as influential in his own hermeneutical project. *Présence au monde* is the grace of understanding deeply one's own times and the capacity to respond accordingly.

For Schillebeeckx, a definitive, final exposition of Christian spirituality cannot be given, since we ourselves are part of the Christian story and it has not thus come to a close. The present provides a new moment in the history of Christian spirituality. A theology of Christian spirituality is valid only insofar as it begins with the story of Jesus and brings that story up to date with one's own times. Any particular Christian spirituality is valid only as a specific modality of "following after Jesus" and only insofar as it has a living relationship to the present. Schillebeeckx's theology can be seen as a bridge between an interpreted historical past and the situation in the world and church today.

Foundational to Schillebeeckx's studies of Jesus, to his reflections on ministry and preaching, to his understanding of church and hermeneutics are, as Lacordaire has put it, the twofold *présence à Dieu* and *présence au monde*. This framework for understanding the spiritual life goes back to Dominic himself, who instructed his own followers to speak only to God or about God. The spiritual life for Schillebeeckx is a parable of God interacting with God's people.

In Schillebeeckx's theology, Christian spirituality is a particular way of being human. It cannot be imposed from the outside or enforced. It never means living "only for God," with little concern for others or our history. Following Jesus can never be a mere repetition of some earlier form of Christian spirituality. Rather, it is a Christian creativity in a historical context. Spirituality is always a new adventure, with Abraham and Sarah as models: "They set out on a journey, not knowing where they were going" (Heb 11:8).

There are two indissoluble elements in Christian praxis: interiority and exteriority, and they belong together; either becomes false if broken away from the other. Spirituality can never be reduced to the inner life and a circle of friends. Such a false spirituality becomes asocial, apolitical, ahistorical, and noncontextual. Christian spirituality is concerned with what it means to be human and thus with the whole social, political, and economic context in which human life is shaped.

Christians are aware that authentic mystical forces will be set free for humanity and greater justice only through an active participation in history. But just as Christian spirituality is not purely mystical inwardness, neither is it simply and only political and social involvement. This "new" spirituality, both contextual and political, is a reflection of Jesus himself, who identified himself with God's concern and identified God's concern with humanity. Spirituality is about God's concern for human beings.

THE EXPERIENCE OF GOD AS *ABBA*

For Schillebeeckx, the center of Jesus' spirituality lies in his experience of God, the "*Abba* experience." With a few exceptions, *Abba* does not occur as a way of addressing God in prayer in the Judaism of Jesus' time. Yet this seems to have been Jesus' habitual way of praying (Mk 14:36). Jesus' way of addressing God in prayer was unconventional, intimate, familial, and indicative of a religious experience of deep intimacy with God that was unique.

Jesus' experience of God was an experience of God as caring and as offering a future to humanity, a God who chose to be identified with the cause of humankind, a God who gave people hope. On the basis of his experience of intimacy with God, "Jesus could bring people the message of a hope which is not to be derived from our world history" (*God Among Us*, p. 88).

Although Jesus' own personal experience of God was unique, his relationship with God was something he envisioned for his disciples. Jesus wanted those who followed after him to have exactly the same relationship with God. The distinction in the fourth gospel between "my Father and your Father" (Jn 20:17) manifests postresurrection Christian theology. Schillebeeckx maintains a distinction between Jesus' experience of God and his disciples' experiences, but not between Jesus' intimate relationship with God and the relationship to God into which he invited his disciples.

The *Abba* experience for Christians is then an experience of God as personal. God challenges and talks with human beings and is even confrontational. In his own spiritual life Schillebeeckx acknowledges personally speaking to God as to a friend. "If you don't talk to God first, you can't talk about him" (*God Is New Each Moment*, p. 125). This latter insight reflects not only Schillebeeckx's Jesus research but also his own appropriation of Dominic's aforementioned exhortation, to "speak only to God or about God."

At the foundation of spirituality, for Schillebeeckx, is Jesus, who is a "parable of God and paradigm of humanity" (*Jesus*, p. 626). Through Jesus we come to know both God and the human being. Thus the secret and source for our own life and ministry must be our own experience of God as the one who cares for us and for humankind, our own continuing intimacy with God in prayer, our own solidarity with God and experience of God as love.

Grace is another foundational theme that permeates Schillebeeckx's writings from his early reflection on Christ as the primordial sacrament *Christ The Sacrament of the Encounter with God* (1963) through the second volume of his project in Christology *Christ* (1980) to his most recent works on ministry *Ministry* (1981), *The Church with a Human Face* (1986). All his writings on christology, the church, sacraments, ministry, and spirituality are an unfolding of a theology of grace, of God as the one who saves, and Jesus Christ as the one through whom salvation is revealed.

Grace in the New Testament (discussed more fully in the previous chapter) means the benevolent, free, merciful, and sovereign love of God for humanity, God's bending toward the human. God is always the one who loves humanity. The whole of the New Testament also affirms that Jesus of Nazareth is the supreme sign of this grace and love. Jesus' life and love to the point of death reveal God as being in solidarity with people, especially with those who suffer and are victims of injustice. "God's name is 'solidarity with my people.' God's own honor lies in the happiness and salvation of humanity" (*Christ*, pp. 639).

God is revealed as a God of human beings. Our relationship with God, grace, renews and re-creates us at the deepest level of our self-identity. Grace is a new possibility for human life, a new mode of human existence. It is a new way of life offered us by God, a call to live community with God and others.

This understanding of grace undergirds two typical ways in which Schillebeeckx speaks about God: God as concerned for humanity and God as new each moment. The chief concern of God is for humankind. God loves us, and our concerns are God's concerns. Already in 1972 Schillebeeckx used this way of speaking about God. "In the life of Jesus it became manifest that his God was a God who is concerned for human beings" (*God Among Us*,

p. 132). This way of speaking about God is so prominent in Schillebeeckx's writings that it is hard to think of any insight more central. Jesus' message of God's rule is centered on the well-being of humankind (see *Jesus*, pp. 237, 239, 240, 241, 652). The connecting link between God and humanity is Jesus. Jesus' cause is God's cause (Jesus' *Abba* experience) and God's cause is the cause of humanity (the proclamation of the reign of God).

This emphasis keeps recurring in Schillebeeckx's essays and homilies. In 1978, he described God's glory as "the happiness and the well-being of humankind in the world" (*God Among Us*, p. 94). In 1979 he wrote, "I am quite clear that to take the part of those in trouble means to follow God himself, God as he has shown his deepest sympathy with human beings in Jesus" (*God Among Us*, p. 114). This way of speaking continues throughout his writings in the eighties (see *God Among Us*, pp. 174, 197, 82).

In addition to the God whose cause is the cause of human beings, Schillebeeckx's God is a constant source of new possibilities. On both counts God is the source of hope. "New possibilities" play a central role in Schillebeeckx's spirituality. The birth of a child is the beginning of a new possibility in our history. This is the basis for belief in eternal life as well: there is no end to the possibilities with which God can surprise us. The future of history remains open. God is always caring and ever new.

The gospel itself can only be handed on through new experiences of it. Schillebeeckx's understanding of tradition is that it is "a living gospel," always new, receptive to those new moments that keep it ever alive, those moments of our own contemporary experience that are something of "a fifth gospel." Tradition calls for new experiences if it is to be handed on as a living reality (see Chapter 3). "*Becoming* a Christian . . . means having one's own life story inscribed in the family story of the Christian community so that as a result one's own life story takes on a new, 'converted,' orientation and at the same time continues the thread of the Christian story in its own way. Insofar as it is truly Christian, action of this kind makes our own life part of a living gospel, a 'fifth' gospel" (*God Among Us*, p. 127).

Our own new experiences of God are part of the living tradition of the gospel that draws us into following after Jesus and the praxis of the reign of God.

FOLLOWING AFTER JESUS

Schillebeeckx's "spirituality" refers not only to our experience of intimacy with God. This experience leads the Christian into following after Jesus. Jesus, whose very own spirituality is thoroughly Jewish, becomes himself the cornerstone of a spirituality for those who came to follow him—both before his resurrection and throughout the centuries since.

Following after Jesus consists in what Schillebeeckx frequently refers to as "the praxis of the reign of God." Indeed, one can say that spirituality for Schillebeeckx is praxis, and specifically orthopraxis. Schillebeeckx defines orthopraxis as action in accord with the reign of God. Orthopraxis, rooted in one's experience of God, is a following of the praxis of Jesus.

Orthopraxis implies an essential relationship between theory and practice. We cannot have one without the other. Schillebeeckx was already insisting upon this in the late 1960s. The basic problem of theology is not that of the relationship between the past (Scripture and tradition) and the present but rather is that of the relationship between theory and practice. How theory manifests itself in praxis is a critical test of the theory. Theology stands under the critical primacy of praxis.

The preoccupation with orthopraxis raises the question of how to bridge the gulf between theory and practice. The earthly Jesus' argument with his coreligionists was not over a lack of orthodoxy but over an attitude in which theory and practice had drifted apart and they had lost sight of God's solidarity with the people. Jesus' refusal to sanction an orthodoxy separated from orthopraxis was the foundation of his critique of Sabbath observance, the Law, and the Temple.

If Christian life or following after Jesus, then, comes down to the praxis of the reign of God, in what does such praxis consist? Only a theology of Jesus reveals this; hence Schillebeeckx's extensive Jesus research. The praxis of the reign of God is manifest in Jesus' proclamation of God's forgiveness and love, in Jesus' healings, in Jesus' table fellowship with outcasts and sinners, in Jesus' approach to the Law, and in his enigmatic parables.

Jesus not only told parables, he was a parable. Jesus is a parable of God in solidarity with people. Jesus' sharing table with the disreputable is symbolic or parabolic action—the praxis of a God whose cause is humanity. Jesus did not oppose Torah or Law. It is simply that the praxis of the reign of God, the praxis to which God calls us, cannot be contained by the Law. Hence the Law, while valid, is relativized by God. As there must be an integral link between theology and practice, so there is an integral link between one's human experience of God and the praxis of the reign of God.

Another fact about Jesus is that he attracted to himself disciples and companions—those who went after him—and that he sent some of them forth to proclaim and practice the coming of God. The praxis of Jesus became that of his disciples, of the post-Easter communities that came together in his name, and eventually of the church. This orthopraxis of Jesus is the criterion by means of which a community or church can name itself Christian. The praxis of the reign of God is constitutive of the nature of the church. "The living community is the only real reliquary of Jesus" (*Christ*, p. 641), for it is in the living community where the praxis of God is continued.

Schillebeeckx's theology is very clearly grounded in human experience. Encountering what it means to follow after Jesus, we are confronted by two contrasting experiences, our experience of God and our experience of suffering.

We have already reflected upon the experience of God. This is God as "pure positivity," who promotes all that is good and opposes all that is evil. As human beings we also have the experience of suffering, even an excess of suffering and evil, "a barbarous excess which resists all explanation and interpretation" (*God Among Us*, p. 149). Theology reflects on our human experience of God and then proceeds to the history of human suffering, which is such a contrast with the purely positive existence that God wills.

What are we to make of this contrast? Jesus' own experience of the contrast had a constructive moment to it, for the contrast experience can offer a moment of critical awareness. The experience of the contrast is at the basis of Jesus' prophetic self-awareness. "Jesus' interpretation of suffering is connected with his deep personal relationship with God, the heart of his life. God and suffering are diametrically opposed; when God appears, evil and suffering have to yield" (*Christ*, p. 695). The experience of contrast yields a critique of the history of suffering and holds forth hope for the future.

The prophet, the theologian, the Christian, all who follow after Jesus must have a "critical memory," the critical memory of this history of human suffering. Although the excess of suffering is an incomprehensible mystery for all, it becomes especially problematic for the person who believes in God. The history of religion and the history of Christian theology have struggled with this memory. One can recall Israel's struggle with suffering and Israel's protest against it, the Hindu insight that each religion is a point of reference pointing to the truth, the Buddhist starting point with the fact of suffering, and even the Enlightenment effort to confront suffering rationally as a problem. Yet in humankind's history there has never been a successful rational theory to account for *all* suffering (suffering is either trivialized or reduced to a particular form of suffering).

Since the powers of human explanation fail when they come up against the history of human suffering, the only meaningful response to this history is to offer resistance. Thus we come back to orthopraxis. In practice, the people of God must refuse to allow evil the right to exist, for God is the author of good and the opponent of evil.

For the person of faith then, the critical memory of human suffering is a contrast experience that results in hope. Jesus' God is a God who *wants* humanity's salvation and a victory over suffering. Christianity, however, does not attempt to explain suffering. Followers of Jesus "do not *argue* against suffering, but tell a *story*" (*Christ*, p. 698), and that story is the story of Jesus: the life, suffering, death, and resurrection of Jesus. Jesus bore witness to a certainty he felt regarding the salvation given by God, that the "making whole" of human life is possible. Faith in Jesus makes it possible to affirm both evil and suffering and also salvation or a final good in a way that allows us to give the last word to well-being and goodness, "because the Father is greater than all our suffering and grief and greater than our inability to experience the deepest reality as in the end a trustworthy gift" (*Jesus*, p. 625).

Given the awareness of the history of human suffering, those who follow Jesus necessarily involve themselves in the struggle for justice. Christian "spirituality" follows a radical integration of the themes of eschatological salvation and human liberation—one theme not to be neglected at the expense of the other, for indeed God's very own foremost concern is humankind.

POLITICAL HOLINESS

Christian love and holiness are necessarily, but not exclusively, a "political love" and a "political holiness." In the struggle against injustice the believer is not only responding to the prior grace and experience of God but also continues to experience the God of Jesus. This political form of love of neighbor is an urgent form of contemporary holiness.

Christianity does not explain suffering. It neither condones injustice nor rationalizes the existing social order. Although Christian history gave rise to a "mysticism of suffering" that emphasized one's personal suffering and in which the cross became a symbol for the legitimation of social abuses, political holiness recognizes Jesus' new definition of holiness as rooted in his new understanding and experience of God. Christian holiness does not legitimate, but opposes injustice because our very understanding of God is at stake.

In Christian life, there is both "a political dimension" and "a mystical dimension" for Schillebeeckx. This integral relationship between mysticism and politics, neither of which can be discounted, is rooted in Jesus who is both paradigm of humanity and parable of God. Both mysticism and politics have the same source: the experience of contrast between God and the history of a suffering humanity.

For the follower of Jesus, the spiritual life cannot be reduced to "personal holiness" alone. Nor can social and political life be reduced to their social and political components alone. For Schillebeeckx, "mysticism" is an intense form of the experience of God or love of God. "Politics" is an intense form of social engagement not restricted to professional politicians. Politics without prayer or mysticism becomes barbaric; mysticism without political love becomes sentimental interiority. A Christian involvement in the world is a *religious* praxis, rooted in a particular interpretation of the world, drawing upon the experience of the holy. "Christian politics" is both specifically religious and also practically effective, making impossible an idealization of any particular form of the world and at the same time forbidding escapism from the world.

Moses, a political leader who brought his people liberation, was a mystic "who spoke to God face to face." For Jesus, the mystical experience of God was the heart and soul of his mission on behalf of the poor. True mysticism has its own intrinsic value, which cannot be located only in its social or political consequences, although true mysticism always does have such consequences. Mysticism can become either a flight into inwardness without social awareness or a prophetic mysticism. "Bourgeois religion" attempts to separate religion and politics, salvation and liberation, whereas authentic Christian salvation implies wholeness. Mystics must become more prophetic and prophets more mystical.

Christian life and spirituality are intimately tied up with one's concept of salvation, and the meaning of salvation has been one of Schillebeeckx's enduring concerns. "Salvation means being whole" (Christ, p. 717), and salvation becomes less than whole if one emphasizes only one dimension of the human—whether this be the sociopolitical or the personal. Social liberation is an integral ingredient of the eschatological salvation offered by God. "Personal salvation" is only partial. Likewise if sociopolitical liberation claims to be total, it becomes a new form of servitude. Human liberation and Christian redemption are not alternatives but are both constitutive elements of Christian hope.

The process of liberation, even without being specifically Christian, can be a form of Christian love. In political questions, faith ought not play too large or too small a role. Christian faith is politically relevant, yet it does not absolutize any political system. The gospel moves Christians toward political action, yet does not of itself present us directly with a specific political program.

As Schillebeeckx's thought continues to develop, notably in his most recent book, On Christian Faith, there is even greater emphasis on the unity of the mystical and the political: the human experience of intimacy with God can be found in the midst of an active love of neighbor.

The mystical dimension of faith itself can take the form of political love. There can be no dualism between interiority and exteriority, between love of God and love of neighbor; nor can one be subordinated to the other. "Love of humanity as a disinterested commitment for fellow human beings is at the same time the hallmark of the truth of love towards God" (*On Christian Faith*, p. 70). Mysticism is possible not only in silence and in contemplation but also in prophetic struggle. At the same time, the active mystic still needs moments of explicit praise and Eucharist.

The dangerous memory of the life and execution and resurrection of Jesus is not only the basis for a liturgical action but also for political action. Christian faith is not neutral with respect to social and political problems, yet Christian faith promotes the autonomy of political reason. Christian faith does not give a blueprint for the economic, social, and political order; these pertain to the art of government, the lessons of history, and the social sciences. At the same time this does not imply that Christian faith and the gospel have nothing to do with the social order. Christian faith has political relevance precisely because Christian salvation implies human liberation. Churches must at all times challenge injustice. Yet social responsibility does not mean that churches take the government of the world into their own hands or that they ally themselves with one particular political or economic system. The gospel provides the basis for a critique of the world, and this includes the social and political structures of the world. Not to criticize actual injustice in a concrete social order is to make a secret compromise with injustice—to which the God of Jesus says "no."

THE SPIRIT, THE CHURCH, AND THE WORLD

Christology is clearly at the center of Schillebeeckx's more recent writings, with the publication of his *Jesus* and *Christ*, but christological concerns undergirded his theology even prior to the Second Vatican Council. In 1959, he had published the Dutch edition of *Christ the Sacrament of the Encounter with God*, which brought into a new focus the profound connections between christology, ecclesiology, the sacraments, and human life. His early theology spoke of a sacrament as an ecclesial act. Jesus Christ is the primordial sacrament of grace. What we ordinarily think of as sacraments are ecclesial acts in which the Christian encounters God as present. These ecclesial concerns continued to be significant as Schillebeeckx took up problematic areas such as lay preaching, liturgy, and ministry, all with an eye toward a deeper understanding of *the human*. His christology, ecclesiology, and spirituality all move with that foundational concern—the desire to specify theologically what it means to be human.

The risen Jesus bestows God's own Spirit, through which the believer enters into a relationship with God and, following after Jesus, into radical service to the world. The world has become as much of a concern to Schillebeeckx as the church. Since the Second Vatican Council, his ecclesial questions relate the church directly to the world.

Being church is ministering to and in the world, but God's salvation is available wherever good is promoted and evil resisted. The church and world cannot be defined in opposition to each other. What is present "outside the church," wherever people give their consent to God's offer of grace, even though they do not do this reflectively or thematically, is audibly expressed and visibly perceptible in the church. "The church must therefore be the sphere where, following Jesus, the praxis of the kingdom of God becomes visible, so that it is clear to everyone through this praxis that despite everything there is ground for hope" (*God Among Us*, p. 120). The church follows after Jesus in the world where such following is a visible sign of hope for the world.

The church is vitally concerned with both mysticism and human liberation. Mysticism, liturgy, and worship without an essential concern for liberation is pseudomysticism, and likewise a church that promotes human liberation but has no mysticism is only half itself. In the church, as in the praxis of Jesus, God and the world come together in such a way that God is seen, experienced, proclaimed, and praised as one whose motivation is the cause of humankind. The church is a community of "people of God" gathered around "the God of people" as revealed in Jesus Christ (*On Christian Faith*, p. 47). God reveals God's very own self as being for the sake of our salvation—which salvation can not be separated from our awareness of the history of human suffering. God, Jesus Christ, and the church are all postured toward the human and have a human face: *Abba*, Son, and Spirit. God is a God who loves humanity.

God's universal love for human beings revealed in the story of Jesus Christ and continuing to be proclaimed through the power of the Spirit increasingly pushes the human (the *humanum*) to center stage in Schillebeeckx's continually developing theology. Salvation is always the salvation of human beings. God's salvation does not turn our gaze away from us, our world, and our human experience. Our God is a God who loves us. An ongoing theological concern for Schillebeeckx is, "In what does salvation consist?" Salvation can never be severed from its relationship to the human. God's very own choice has been for an authentic humanism, a religious humanism, even a "humanism of the rejected." Christian salvation comprises both God's redemptive acts and the human historical struggle for liberation. Salvation, however, cannot identify itself with either one to the exclusion of the other. God is always and absolutely for humanity.

Christian salvation is meant as salvation *from God,* but *for human beings.* Thus Christian salvation and Christian spirituality are concerned with human beings becoming human. Salvation or spirituality cannot be related solely to a personal holiness alone, or to political or ecological appeals alone, or to an eschatological hope alone, or to a nonhistorical or mystical perspective alone to the exclusion of the other aspects of the human. Christian salvation for Schillebeeckx is not simply a matter of "saving souls." Salvation must be experienced by concrete human beings as saving. Salvation refers to human wholeness, human well-being in all its dimensions. It implies the solidarity of Christians with the processes of human liberation even when the church has nothing in particular to gain from the liberation movement.

Defining the content of full human liberation remains impossible. It is that toward which we strive. In the end it involves the presence of the living God in the lives of the people and the presence of the people in their history and world.

Christian spirituality is concerned with what it means to be human. In the end, it is a theology of the human. Jesus is paradigmatic of the human, and Jesus discloses that being human or being whole involves both an experience of God as intimate and also the praxis of the reign of God. Authentic Christian praxis is both mystical and political. Political love or the political shape that love of neighbor necessarily takes in our world today constitutes a particular understanding of holiness—an image of God as a God of people, a God whose concern is humanity. To be holy is to be concerned with human beings. Holiness never legitimates an escape from the world but rather necessitates presence to the world and its struggles for human liberation.

The human, which is God's innermost concern, is not definitively definable and is only fragmentarily found. It is best expressed in symbolic language or metaphorical speech. Three great metaphors from the New Testament suggest the complete *humanum* (*God Among Us*, pp. 161–62). First is the definitive salvation or radical liberation of all men and women for a sisterly and brotherly community or society that is no longer dominated by master-servant relationships: the metaphor of the reign of God. Second is the complete salvation and happiness of the individual person within this society: the metaphor of the resurrection of the flesh. Third is the perfection of the ecological environment necessary for human life: the biblical idea of the new heaven and the new earth.

Again we are reminded that spirituality is not just one aspect of human life that can be singled out. It is the whole of human life and the making of human life whole. It is following the praxis of Jesus, the praxis of the reign of God, an orthopraxis both deeply mystical and necessarily political. It is an intimate involvement with a God who loves people.

SUGGESTIONS FOR FURTHER READING

The most complete collection of Schillebeeckx's homilies, essays, and lectures in the area of spirituality is found in *God Among Us: The Gospel Proclaimed*. To explore further the aspects of Schillebeeckx's approach to spirituality highlighted in this chapter see especially "Jesus the Prophet," pp. 33–44; "You Are the Light of the World (Luke 2:19–32)," pp. 85–90; "I Believe in the Man Jesus: The Christ, the Only Beloved Son, Our Lord," pp. 103–15; "Liberation from Panic (Easter Faith)," pp. 122–27; "Introverted or Turned Towards the World?" pp. 164–74; "How Shall We Sing the Lord's Song in a Strange Land? (Ps. 137:4)," pp. 180–87; and "Dominican Spirituality," pp. 232–48.

For the fuller Christological foundations of Schillebeeckx's spirituality see *Jesus*, especially pp. 229–71. Schillebeeckx's discussion of God's opposition to human suffering can be found in

Christ, pp. 670–743. His understanding of "political holiness" and the relationship between mysticism and politics as well as liturgy and social justice can be traced in *Christ*, pp. 762–821, and *On Christian Faith*, pp. 47–84.

Parts V and VI of *The Schillebeeckx Reader* contain significant excerpts from Schillebeeckx's writings on the relationship of church and world and spirituality, some portions of which cannot be found elsewhere in English translation. An easily read introduction to Schillebeeckx, which offers rich insight into his own spirituality, is his conversation recorded in *God Is New Each Moment*.

7. Salvation in and for the World: Church and Sacraments

SUSAN A. ROSS

"The world and the human history in which God wills to bring about salvation for men and women are the basis for the whole reality of salvation. . . . There is no salvation, not even any religious salvation, outside the human world" (*On Christian Faith*, p. 8). This quotation, striking in its emphasis on the concrete context of human religious life, is an apt one to introduce Edward Schillebeeckx's theology of church and sacraments, for it sums up his understanding of the relation between the sacred and the secular. It is in those institutions and practices that symbolize the sacred to the world—the church and the sacraments—that this concrete emphasis is needed more than anywhere else. And while his theology has changed in content and style over the forty-plus years of his publications, Schillebeeckx's concern for the concrete and historical life of the church has been a constant one.

Schillebeeckx first became known to American audiences through the publication of his book *Christ the Sacrament of the Encounter with God* in 1963. In that work, Schillebeeckx wrote how our life with God is rooted in our life in the world: "Life itself in the world then belongs to the very content of God's inner word to us. . . . Life itself becomes a truly supernatural and external revelation . . ." (p. 8). Over twenty years later, the same ideas are reflected: "Thus there is an indissoluble bond between religion and world. God cannot be reached outside his own manifestations and he never coincides with any one of them" ("Jeruzalem of Benares? Nicaragua of de Berg Athos?" 1983, cited in *The Schillebeeckx Reader*, p. 257).

The church and the sacraments are the places where humanity's relationship with God is given concrete form: in institutional structures, in liturgical celebrations, and in all the ways in which Christians explicitly acknowledge their faith in the salvation proclaimed by Jesus. This concern for the relation between the church and the world and the concrete ways in which this relationship is expressed is a thread that runs through all of Schillebeeckx's work. What marks the difference between the earlier and the later works is an ever more vivid concern with the structures of contemporary human existence and the real problems human beings face in living their lives. The unity in all of Schillebeeckx's writings is found in his focus on the concrete and historical dimensions of life as the place of God's revelation to humankind.

CONCRETENESS AND HISTORICITY

What does it mean to live in the "concrete"? We human beings do not live in the abstract. We live in the world, in families, in friendships, in nations, and we relate to each other and to the world itself through our bodies, our social institutions, and our histories. We are body-bound people. We come to know each other through the distinctive ways we are present to one another: color of hair, tone of voice, gesture or touch. Of course, we know that who we are is much more than what we look like or sound like (although, tragically, racism, sexism, and other forms of discrimination continue to plague our lives). But we cannot "step out of our skins" as if we were *really* souls who just happen to occupy bodies for the present. Our embodiedness is part and parcel of our existence.

We are also people of history: of particular times and places. We are conditioned by the kind of parents we had, the kind of education we receive, and the culture in which we live. We are increasingly aware of how our place in time and space determines, in great part, how we react to events, how we interpret them, and the meaning we give to them. Although there are issues that concern human existence over time (Schillebeeckx calls these "anthropological constants, permanent human impulses and orientations"), these issues are always situated within a context and have different implications in different times and places. As we cannot step out of our bodies, neither can we step out of time.

The fact that we are embodied, that we live in particular times and places, is crucial for Schillebeeckx. It is here, in our existence, that we encounter God. Like his contemporary Karl Rahner, Schillebeeckx does not separate the "natural" from the "supernatural" order; both are in fact all part of one "supernatural," graced order. We encounter God in and through our experiences as human beings. Concreteness and historicity are then the basis for sacramentality and the mode of the church's existence in the world.

This sacramentality is, in the Christian tradition, centered in the person of Jesus. God's ultimate self-revelation is found in the completely human life of Jesus of Nazareth, for whom "God's lordship is not just an idea or theory, but first and foremost an experience of reality" (*Jesus*, p. 142). Salvation is the experience of God's concern as rooted and enacted in our human life. This means, then, that salvation has concrete and historical dimensions that become realized in human life: in other words, it is sacramental.

From the earliest years of his theological career, Schillebeeckx has sought to remind us that the sacraments are not simply "pipelines" for God's grace, but rather that they emerge out of concrete human experiences by which we understand ourselves as related to and transformed by God's salvation. The key for Schillebeeckx is the recognition of the sacraments in the context of our experiences as human beings. So when we speak of the church as sacrament or of the sacraments themselves as signs of sacred realities, we must reflect on what the church actually represents, how our experience reveals God's grace. Too easily we may be led into taking a mechanical approach to the sacraments, which emphasizes what they do ("give grace") without understanding what that grace actually means in our lives. We need to understand what it is that salvation in Jesus means for us, now, in the latter years of the twentieth century.

The church is the place where this salvation is explicitly recognized, professed, and celebrated. It is the community of believers who "stand in the tradition of Israel and Jesus of Nazareth" (*On Christian Faith*, p. 41). The church exists in the world as a sign, or sacrament, of salvation, but Schillebeeckx is careful to point out that the church is not identical with salvation itself: "We may not identify the existing churches with the kingdom of God" (*On*

Christian Faith, p. 44). We need, on the one hand, to beware of "ecclesiocentrism" (the church existing for itself) and, on the other, a dismissal of the church's relevance in an increasingly secular world. It is in the church's distinctive actions—prayer, ritual, ethics—that the message of salvation is kept alive in the world.

The biblical understanding of salvation is always related to particular situations. It is never purely internal or addressed only to the individual. Salvation is found in human experiences of "redemption, liberation, renewal of life, happiness, and fulfillment" (*Christ*, p. 464). Here we find God's solidarity with humanity, affirmed in both Old and New Testaments, against all those forces (social, psychological, spiritual) that work against the happiness of human beings. In the world today, this may take the form of "liberation" movements, as we see in Latin American and other Third World liberation theologies. Or it may take the form of communities that criticize the oppression of people within the church itself. Wherever there is suffering or injustice, God's message of salvation stands against it.

Jesus' own understanding of salvation, of liberation from suffering, was spoken in the language of the "kingdom of God": "For Jesus the kingdom is to be found where human life becomes 'whole,' where 'salvation' is realized for men and women, where righteousness and love begin to prevail, and enslaving conditions come to an end" (*The Church With a Human Face*, p. 20). For Schillebeeckx, "salvation" is then a concrete and historical reality (and is therefore sacramental). Rooted in the Scriptures, expressed in the life and teachings of Jesus of Nazareth, salvation means God's presence in our struggles against suffering—the "barbarous excess" (*Christ*, p. 725) of suffering, injustice, and misery in human life.

Human existence for the Christian today is where *we* make human life whole, where righteousness and love are present *now*, where we are reconciled with the meaning and end of our existence. As our existence is social as well as embodied, communal as well as historical, it is in the church that God's message of salvation is expressed.

THE CHURCH AS SACRAMENT

Schillebeeckx's interest in the church has been a constant throughout his career. In *Christ the Sacrament of the Encounter with*

God, he emphasized the importance of the "community of the faithful" as well as that of the more often emphasized (especially in preconciliar years) hierarchical church. But it was during the years of the Second Vatican Council (1962–1965) that Schillebeeckx came to a more critical understanding of the church as community. This understanding has only intensified over the years, especially as Schillebeeckx has devoted more time to studying the historical roots of the church and by relating this history to the present. It is also a concern that has brought him into conflict with the hierarchical authorities of the church.

What do we mean by "church"? Surely we mean more than the buildings and institutions that bear the name of church, and we mean not only those in authority. The church is even more than the specific community of believers that bears the name "Christian." To put it in the broadest possible terms, the church is the active presence of God's salvation in the world—or, as Schillebeeckx put it in his earlier writings, the church is the "sacrament of the world."

As sacrament, the church is a concrete and historical institution. This means that it is made up of human beings united in their belief in the salvation brought by Jesus and that it also exists in time and space, influenced by the cultures of which it is a part. Yet the church is also not "merely" another human institution, like the Federal Reserve Bank or the University of Chicago. As the church is the active presence of God's salvation in the world—a salvation that brings justice, hope, and wholeness to human beings—it is not limited to the social and institutional structures of the visible reality we call "the church." The church is present implicitly, if not visibly, where justice is done, where humans are working for the liberation of all the people. Therefore we can say, in the words of the third-century bishop Cyprian, "There is no salvation outside the church," while we recognize that the church's boundaries are not limited to any one institution, least of all only to the Roman Catholic church. Schillebeeckx is keenly aware of the Catholic church's tendency in the past to identify itself with the kingdom of God and to fail to see God's word outside Roman Catholicism and Christianity. One of the most positive contributions of the Second Vatican Council is that of the call for a dialogue that recognizes the integrity of other religious traditions. Thus the church is called on to listen as well as speak, to convert itself from the triumphalist attitudes of the past, and to be constantly self-critical. This call for self-criticism becomes a constant refrain in Schillebeeckx's writings on the church from Vatican II on.

From the very beginning of its existence, the church has tried to understand itself and its mission in continuity with the message of Jesus Christ. This message has always had social implications and was never "only" a message concerning the individual person alone. But there was no "blueprint" left for the church by Jesus, no "plan" that outlined exactly how the church was to govern itself, how it ought to respond to certain situations. As the early communities grew, various forms of church leadership and order developed as responses to the needs of the communities. And these developments took on their own existence as time progressed.

THE DEVELOPMENT OF THE CHURCH

In one of the most provocative sections of *The Church with a Human Face*, Schillebeeckx says, "One can say that the communities of God which came into being on the basis of the resurrection of Jesus are what is meant *at the deepest level* in the New Testament by 'the appearances of Jesus'" (p. 34). The Christian communities are themselves the places where Jesus' message of salvation and liberation remains living, and this message was then and remains today the standard by which the church is judged.

The early church attempted to live out its understanding of the message of salvation by discerning where, in its own tradition and in its own culture, one could best live out Jesus' message. In the earliest years of the church's existence, for example, one understanding of church was as a "pneumatic," Spirit-filled church: this Christian community understood itself to live in "the fullness of time," and consequently it saw the world outside as "irrelevant." Each member of the community saw himself or herself as inspired by the Spirit and as freed from the distinctions of "the world" (such as race, gender, or civil status). But this Spirit-filled, egalitarian sense of church eventually gave way to an understanding of itself that emphasized a greater sense of order and authority.

Over time, the structures of church order established by the members of the church became more and more centralized, as Schillebeeckx carefully shows in his books on ministry. The development of church order (of leadership, of the nature of bishops, priests, and laity) grew in accordance with the way that the church saw itself *at that time,* attempting to live out the message of salvation. These various structures of order, themselves "adaptations of a religion to its cultural environment" (*The Church with a Human Face,* p. 69) became, over time, identified with the religion itself.

When this happens—when the historical structure becomes identified with the message of salvation—the limitations of the historical structure become evident, conflict arises, and new forms of church order emerge to respond to the needs of a new situation. Schillebeeckx's work on ministry is both a description and evaluation of these forms of church order as they developed over the course of two millennia of Christianity. Schillebeeckx's goal, as a theologian, is to reflect on both theological and historical/cultural factors in Christian ecclesiology (the study of what it means to be church) and to remind the church of and sometimes confront it with its reliance on the message of Jesus. How do various forms of church order convey this message? First we must be able to interpret and judge the church *theologically:* how is it faithfully living out the reality of God's message of salvation? Then we must look at it *historically:* how does this or that particular action of the church represent God's kingdom now? The *theological* meaning is always found within the historical, in the concrete. To judge the church only on theoretical grounds is not only to ignore the church's own situation in time and space but it is also, as Schillebeeckx points out in *The Church with a Human Face,* "untrue to the gospel" (p. 5). But to judge the church only on historical or cultural grounds is to reduce the reality of the church to a "mere" historical phenomenon. To fall into either extreme is to fail to see the *sacramentality* of the church: that God's grace is to be found *within* human experience.

It is from this perspective that Schillebeeckx takes on the issue of infallibility: how the church can speak "without error" on matters of faith. The term "infallibility" is itself a part of a historical context, Schillebeeckx reminds us. And ever mindful of this historicity and the historical context of any statement of faith (and therefore its relative and not absolute claim to the truth), Schillebeeckx argues that the church can, in specific situations, speak correctly and faithfully on issues of Christian faith. This "correctness" is never to be taken in a triumphalist sense but is rather to be seen as a process of constantly witnessing to the truth in conversion and self-criticism.

THE CHURCH AS CRITICAL COMMUNITY

As we have already seen in previous chapters (especially Chapter 2, "Interpretation and Method"), the philosophical and sociological movement of "critical theory" has had a deep influence on Schillebeeckx. In his consideration of the church, critical theory plays an important role.

Insofar as the church is a social and historical reality, it is open to criticism on both historical and theological grounds. Therefore, Schillebeeckx sees the role of the theologian as continually reminding and confronting the church to be conscious of its own interests: the community of believers in the service of the message of Jesus. This means that new situations can and do give rise to new expressions of the ongoing faith of the church. These new expressions, however, inevitably collide with the human reality of the church, and the established order of the church—a historical reality—can become rigid and resistant to change. Indeed, this rigidity can and in fact has, over the course of church history, "become fixed as an ideology and itself hinders the original purpose of the church" (*Ministry*, p. 79).

For Schillebeeckx, this is where we see the importance of "critical communities" in the church. These communities are critical not only of unjust structures in society but also of those within the church. Based in the local community, these groups strive to live out the message of the kingdom by confronting injustice wherever it is found and by developing new forms of community that respond to the needs of the present day.

This understanding of church as "critical community" has arisen out of a deep sense of humanity's (and therefore also the church's) historicity. It also comes from a new understanding of Jesus. Schillebeeckx's years of study of biblical material (which resulted in his massive volumes *Jesus* and *Christ*) has had a deep impact on his own understanding of church. He himself has become more critical of the church's tendency to isolate itself within its hierarchical structures. Consequently, Schillebeeckx has come to place great importance on the ways in which present-day Christians are responding to the need for salvation in their own lives and in their own communities. Some of these ways are resulting in practices that are regarded as "illegal" by the hierarchical church, insofar as they violate official church law. The continuation of ministerial practice by married priests and the leadership of the Eucharist by the nonordained are examples of new ways of living out one's commitment to the message of Jesus that speak from a new and different *theology* of church, of ministry, of Eucharist. This theology comes out of critical reflection on experience and an openness to new experiences to discern how God is working in human life today. For Schillebeeckx, these new experiences have an "authority" as they reveal our liberation from oppressive structures even within the church. Schillebeeckx is then especially sensitive to the current "shortage" of priests despite the willingness of men and women willing to work in church ministries and yet unwilling or unable to accept the present conditions for ordination. Schillebeeckx's language has become increasingly sharp and critical; the temptations of the church to become sectarian, clericalist, and apolitical are all too great.

Indeed, such has been Schillebeeckx's critical concern that it has brought him into conflict with the official teaching office of the church—the magisterium. Between 1976 and 1979, Schillebeeckx's work in christology was the subject of an investigation by the magisterium, and this experience has prompted Schillebeeckx to rethink his understanding of the role of the magisterium in the life of the church. The role of the magisterium is to judge whether or not expressions of faith adequately reflect the church's scriptural and theological tradition in the light of contemporary experience. The magisterium thus has a judicial function and it has the power to "silence" a theologian (as it has done in the case of Leonardo Boff). For Schillebeeckx, the magisterium's recent actions are of concern because they have not allowed for a "mutually critical confrontation of the tradition of faith" and contemporary experience, arguing instead for "clarity" at the expense of the metaphorical language of faith ("Theologische overpeinzing achteraf," in *Schillebeeckx Reader*, pp. 95–97). This "mutually critical correlation" is a difficult process, but a necessary one, if there is to be genuine discussion and even argument in the struggle to develop ever more adequate expressions of Christian faith. As Schillebeeckx sees it, the role of the magisterium should be to encourage fruitful exchange among theologians, the laity, and the episcopacy and to encourage greater theological understanding on the part of the laity. Its judicial functions should be open rather than secret, and its mission should be one of mutual exchange and discussion rather than that of condemnation.

Consequently, Schillebeeckx's understanding of the church has taken on more critical and specific forms, which in contemporary society means a greater attention to the political realities encountered in the world. There is an inherent tension in the church's situation in the world: while it reveals the kingdom of God, it is not a pure and complete revelation, but one that is partial, somewhat hidden, and incomplete. Despite this incompleteness, the church is a beacon of God's message to suffering humanity. Therefore it is imperative that the church ally itself with the struggle to overcome this suffering. As Schillebeeckx puts it in a 1973 essay, "In contemporary society, it is impossible to believe in a Christianity that is not at one with the movement to emancipate humankind" ("Critical Theories and Christian Political Commitment").

SACRAMENTS AS ENCOUNTER WITH GOD

For Schillebeeckx, "sacrament" was the central concern of his theology in the 1950s and 1960s. His first works published outside of the Netherlands, his book on Christ as primordial sacrament, his two-volume work on marriage, and his writings on eucharistic presence were (and are) major contributions to Christian theology and to the contemporary discussions on sacramental changes in the liturgical life of the church. As his attention has become more and more oriented to this interpretation of our present experience, critical theory, and biblical exegesis, it might appear that sacrament is no longer a serious concern for

Schillebeeckx. A closer look at Schillebeeckx's work since Vatican II, however, shows that a concern for sacraments remains significant in the present, although the context of this concern has shifted.

In the last twenty years, the importance and meaningfulness of human life in all its dimensions—especially a recognition of the "secular"—has been a dominant theme in Schillebeeckx's writings. The increasing secularization of our world, while viewed with dismay by some, is not a cause for alarm for Schillebeeckx. Indeed this increasing awareness of our worldliness is a reminder of our need to concern ourselves not only with the so-called spiritual needs of people, but also with *all* of our human ("material" *or* "spiritual") needs. This recognition of the secular means that our attitude toward the sacraments needs to be refocused.

We need to be aware of two possible extremes in the way we understand God's presence in human life as found in the sacraments. One extreme is to see the sacraments (and, by implication, the church) as a haven for the sacred in the midst of a hostile, secular world. Church and sacraments then become isolated from the world, contrasted with the world as the place where one encounters God—and nowhere else! It was, in part, to this distorted way of thinking that much of Schillebeeckx's early work on sacraments was addressed: his goal was to emphasize the rootedness of sacraments within the experiences of our common human life.

But we need to be aware of another possible extreme, which is to say that sacramental life is merely a vague and implicit awareness of God's presence in secular life, as if our experience of God were "brought down to the level of a pleasant little chat consisting of 'good morning' and 'have a nice weekend' " (*God the Future of Man*, p. 113). What is missing in this misinterpretation of sacramental life is an awareness of and an expression of God's transforming love within human life: here it becomes only a "trivial commonplace."

If we take seriously our human lives as the place of encounter with God and the sacraments as the symbolic celebration of that encounter, then we need to take seriously the conditions of our lives, which are marked by despair and suffering, but also by hope, for in the message of Jesus, which declares that "God's cause is the human cause," we know that our suffering and despair are not the last word. The sacraments are where we publicly declare and celebrate this hope.

SACRAMENTS AS ANTICIPATORY SIGNS

If sacraments are symbols of salvation, then they are symbols of what our lives might be as healed and reconciled: "They are symbols of protest serving to unmask the life that is not yet reconciled in the specific dimensions of our history" (*Christ*, p. 836). The sacraments and the church's liturgy are symbols that make present and keep alive the hope for salvation, which is not yet accomplished in our midst.

This hope cannot be relegated to political action alone, although political action is not irrelevant to our sacramental lives. The human need for symbolic expression—indeed the realization that our embodiedness is itself a symbol of our transcendence—must be met in an understanding of self and existence as graced and in the concrete implications of this graced existence. The entire sacramental life of the church is then a recognition of God's saving presence among suffering humanity. Each individual sacrament provides a focused way of encountering God's liberating action in human life.

Schillebeeckx's understanding of the individual sacraments is concerned both with their own histories in the church and with their significance in the light of our present-day experience. We need to understand sacramental history so that we can be aware of the origin of particular practices and their relevance—or possible irrelevance—for the present. As Schillebeeckx so often points out, we need to be cautious lest our historical forms become fossilized and lose their potential to be "anticipatory signs" of salvation.

Baptism and confirmation, our sacraments of initiation, mark our entry into and commitment to the message of Christian hope. As initiatory practices, they can be interpreted along anthropological lines, as the cultural anthropologist Victor Turner would in calling them "rites of passage." But these "rites" in the Christian tradition—originally the one sacrament of the baptism of the Spirit—have a special significance in that they are signs of our unity with the Spirit, who fills us with life and leads us in the ways of salvation. Confirmation is our adult acknowledgment and renewal of our commitment to our lives as Christians. It recommits us to the struggle to overcome the structures of oppression.

Penance is also a way of discerning God's presence in human life: here, in the acknowledgement that Christian life is not always lived as it should be. We who have been baptized fail to live according to our promises; reconciliation is how we actually and symbolically are reconciled to the community that gives us life. The sacrament of the sick symbolizes our need for healing, physically and spiritually. Here the suffering of humanity is acknowledged: our illnesses, our nearness to death. In this sacrament, our very real suffering is heard, attended to, comforted. The changes in sacramental practice since Vatican II, which emphasize both the social and the individual contexts of sin in the sacrament of reconciliation and the healing quality of the sacrament of the sick, are ways in which we show that the present experience of Christians is addressed by changes in sacramental practice.

The sacrament of Orders (which will be discussed extensively in the next chapter) is the subject of much historical work on the part of Schillebeeckx. His description of how the charisms of the early church became concentrated in the leadership of the church and, ultimately, in the cultic priesthood is a fascinating and involved story. The diversity of ministries in the early church (mission, catechesis, prophecy, and liturgy), which eventually became centralized in the person of the priest, the development of the hierarchy, and the medieval movement toward the "ritualistic priest"—all were responses made by communities through their own cultural "filters" to the call for leadership (a need of *any* social institution). The present "crisis" surrounding the priesthood and the sacrament of Orders is for Schillebeeckx a signal that the traditional understanding of priesthood *must* change to respond to present needs. The recognition that celibacy was a fourth-century development concerning abstinence and "ritual purity," that the prohibition against extending the sacrament to women is an unjust exclusion that had historical origins (themselves questionable, as feminist exegetes have pointed out)—this knowledge of our history is at the same time a call to recognize the "authority of new experiences" and thus a new understanding of Orders and ministry.

Marriage was the subject of an extensive study by Schillebeeckx with a telling title: *Marriage: Human Reality and Saving Mystery.* In this work, Schillebeeckx's skill as a historical theologian is again evident as he shows how the last in the history of the sacraments evolved over time as a response to human needs in particular situations. Throughout this study, Schillebeeckx emphasizes the integrity of the "secular reality" of marriage: "fully human and consequently subject to development and evolution" (*Marriage*, p. 397). This secular reality is sacramental: it is the way in which two persons who have committed their lives to each other encounter God. Yet despite its sacramental character, marriage has, over time, been seen as a "lesser" calling than the "higher" one of a religious life. The "canonically compulsory coupling" (*The Church with a Human Face*, p. 254) of ministry and celibacy in the Roman Catholic tradition is, for Schillebeeckx, a historically conditioned reality that is not, in the present, an adequate answer to the needs of the church.

Eucharist, the pinnacle of our liturgical life as Christians, has also been studied extensively by Schillebeeckx. He was a part of the lively debates in the 1960s concerning the "real presence" of Christ in the Eucharist and the appropriateness of the concept of "transubstantiation" to describe the presence of Christ in the sacrament. Schillebeeckx's emphasis in his lectures to the bishops at Vatican II (later published as *The Eucharist*) was on the historical development of that concept, and in his work since he has been critical of any sense of "localized" or "magical" presence within the bread and wine—a tendency that goes back to a medieval symbol system that no longer makes sense in our world. Jesus is rather present in the community that makes his presence "real." God is *always* present to us—even if we do not always make ourselves present to God!—and as we open ourselves to this presence and act upon it, we make God's salvation present in our lives, in the lives of others, and in the world.

All of the sacraments direct our attention to the concrete and historical message of salvation. While the sacraments and the liturgy dramatize, represent, and challenge us with the message of God's alliance with us, they are completed only in our entire lives, when we are involved in "liberating action in our world" (*Christ*, p. 836).

As sacrament, the church is found wherever we commit ourselves to making Jesus' message of the kingdom of God a reality in our lives. The sacraments are our inspiration and celebration of this commitment. In church and sacrament, we keep alive what is not fully realized yet: "For as long as salvation and peace are still not actual realities, hope for them must be attested and above all nourished and kept alive. . ." (*Christ*, p. 836).

SUGGESTIONS FOR FURTHER READING

Schillebeeckx's interest in sacraments is especially prominent in his writings in the 1950s and 1960s. *Christ the Sacrament of the Encounter with God* remains a very important work because of Schillebeeckx's reworking of the traditional categories of Thomas Aquinas in personalist, existential terms. *The Eucharist* and *Marriage: Human Reality and Saving Mystery* show Schillebeeckx's though on particular sacraments and his continuing interest in and concern for the ongoing history of the sacramental tradition.

His 1971 book of essays, *World and Church*, shows Schillebeeckx's transition from the scholastic language of church and sacrament to a more humanistic approach. One might compare "Priest and Layman in a Secular World" with some of the ideas presented in the two ministry books, *Ministry: Leadership in the Community of Jesus Christ* and *The Church with a Human Face*. "Secular Worship and Church Liturgy," in *God the Future of Man*, is a forthright response to the charge of "irrelevance" by the "secular" theologians of the 1960s and shows Schillebeeckx's increasing involvement in "secular" issues as they affect the church.

In the last section of *Christ: The Experience of Jesus as Lord*, Schillebeeckx reflects on the meaning of sacraments as "anticipatory symbols" and also includes as an epilogue a creed and a eucharistic prayer that eloquently convey in liturgical language the depth of Schillebeeckx's sacramental concerns.

8. The Praxis of the Kingdom of God: Ministry

MARY E. HINES, S.N.D.

It is widely agreed that there is a crisis in ministry today. There are too few priests; communities are being deprived of the Eucharist for long periods of time; the permanence of the priestly vocation as well as the universal requirement of celibacy are questioned. On the other hand, the laity, women and men, married and single, are offering themselves in increasing numbers for pastoral service in the church, including the service of leadership. Women, in particular, question the restriction of eucharistic presidency to celibate men. Some Christian communities experiment with alternative ministerial practices that depart from existing church order. Is this crisis a dangerous assault on the church's tradition? Or is it a significant opportunity for the church's understanding of ministry to expand and adapt to meet today's needs?

The Church with a Human Face, Schillebeeckx's most recent contribution to this discussion, will be the focus of this chapter (quotations used are from this work unless otherwise noted). This work expands and clarifies *Ministry*, his earlier book on the subject. The new work was prompted, at least in part, by a desire to respond to certain criticisms brought to bear against *Ministry* both by some theologians and by the magisterium. In response to these critiques, in *The Church with a Human Face* Schillebeeckx clarifies his methodological presuppositions more carefully, organizes the theological material more tightly, and nuances the historical section. Thus this book provides a good synthesis of his most recent and developed thought on the topic. Before presenting this thought, a possible point of confusion for English readers needs to be clarified. Although the term "ministry," used in the English translations of both works, conveys in present usage a wide variety of services in the Christian community, the Dutch term it translated refers more narrowly to the service of leadership. Schillebeeckx's main focus in these works is office in the church or the evolution of and present concerns about the ordained ministry, although he does touch on some aspects of the wider discussion.

Schillebeeckx's work on ministry is an excellent example of the distinctive methodology he has developed over the course of his long theological career. He begins with the present-day praxis of ministry in the church. He finds there negative experiences leading to the crisis described above. "The dominant conceptions about the practice and the theology of ministry seem to be robbing the gospel of its force in communities of believers" (p. 1).

In the face of these problems of contemporary praxis, Schillebeeckx looks for "contrast experiences" that will provide possibilities for diagnoses of present-day ills and point toward their solution for the future. He turns to the data of history for these contrast experiences—not to retrieve or repeat one particular historical solution, but to point to a pattern of response to changing social and cultural situations.

In line with a key principle of his theology, that revelation takes place through history, Schillebeeckx finds the normative principle for ministry in the variety of forms that it has taken through history. No one particular period should be considered the absolute norm, whether it be New Testament ministry or the modern image of the priest.

With today's questions in mind Schillebeeckx looks back at the various manifestations of the church's understanding of its ministry in differing historical periods. He looks at the rootedness of ministry in the message of the life, death, and resurrection of Jesus and the messianic communities in which that message and ministry were continued. He then considers the practice and theology of ministry in the earliest communities from both what he calls sociohistorical and theological perspectives. Finally, before turning once again to the contemporary questions that prompt the inquiry, he surveys the development of the organization and spirituality of ministry throughout the course of church history. In each of these periods he finds the practice and understanding of ministry adapting to specific social, cultural, and spiritual needs of the time.

The changes in ministry he observes Schillebeeckx character-
izes as "legitimate but not necessary." In other words ministerial
responses arose out of the human choice to actualize some possibilities rather than others. There is a normativity in the sacramental nature of Christian ministry, but this cannot be abstracted
from the concrete historical situation in which it is imbedded.
Historical choices remain contingent and changeable. Later periods are not absolutely bound by any one historical solution but by
the principle that change and development are necessary if fidelity to the gospel message is to be preserved in different social and
cultural situations.

These convictions rest on Schillebeeckx's absolute opposition
to the dualism often assumed between "above" (that which comes
directly from God through Jesus Christ) and "below" (that which
is perceived to arise from the human choices of the Christian
community). He overcomes this dualism through his resolutely
sacramental understanding of the Christian community. The
Christian community is the place where the Spirit of the risen
Christ continues to dwell. Thus there can be no talk of *merely* human or historical responses in the Christian community or of a
purely functional ministry "from below." On the contrary, because of Schillebeeckx's profound conviction of the indwelling of
the Spirit in the community, he is convinced that what comes
"from below" at the same time comes "from above." It is precisely through the decisions of the sacramental, human, historical
community that God acts in the world.

This same conviction also leads him to critique a presupposi-
tion he says lies behind what he calls the "classical" view of the
priest. This view presumes, implicitly at least, that Jesus Christ
was a priest on the basis of his divine, not his human, nature. If
the church's ministry is a sharing in the ministry of Christ, which
Schillebeeckx regards as correct, this view has led to a problematic "sacral ontologizing" of the ministry. Schillebeeckx proposes
that a view of ministry that takes seriously the humanity of Jesus
as a basis for priesthood is truer to the nature of Christian sacramentalism and overcomes the dualism present in the classical
view. If Jesus is the primordial sacrament, it is precisely because *as
human* he is fullest revelation of the divine. A true sacramentalism
cannot bypass the humanity of Jesus. Once again this underlines

Schillebeeckx's emphasis on the fact that God's revelation comes to us *through* the human and historical. There is no dichotomy between a vertical and a horizontal understanding of revelation and thus there is none between an "above" and a "below" understanding of the development of ministry. And there is no dualism between a Christological and a pneumatic-ecclesial understanding of ministry. It is *in* the pneumatic-ecclesial community that one finds the Christological foundations of ministry.

In the light of this conviction Schillebeeckx approaches the historical material from a sociohistorical as well as theological perspective and shows the interrelatedness of these approaches to the same data. Both are in service of the search for the manifestation of the grace of God in history. "There is no surplus of revelation above or in addition to specific historical forms" (p. 11).

The hermeneutical principle governing Schillebeeckx's use of the historical texts is that one goes to the texts with the questions raised by the contemporary practice of ministry, including what he refers to as "illegal practices." These questions provide the horizon for interrogating the texts. There is thus no such thing as an entirely neutral reading of history. This is not to say, however, that one approaches a text merely with the purpose of justifying a particular practice or church structure. Rather one should read the texts with an openness to being illumined by the practice of the past and particularly with the possibility of discovering there some forgotten truths that might help in the assessment of today's practice.

He advocates a dialectical process between past and present that allows one to investigate whether "the actual practice of Christians and Christian communities is for the time being simply a possible sign of faith; . . . [or] whether it is a real sign of faith" (p. 11). In this dialectical process one discovers in history "contrast experiences" that allow one to ask whether a particular exercise of ministry today is positive or negative. The praxis of contemporary Christian communities also serves a diagnostic purpose in exposing possible ideology in existing systems of ministry. The fundamental question is: "Are the specific forms of ministry given in history liberating or enslaving and alienating for the believing community?" (p. 12). This process can then illuminate and provide the basis for a critical assessment of today's practice of ministry and point to some directions for the future exercise of ministry in the church.

THE DATA FROM HISTORY

Schillebeeckx begins his historical investigation with Jesus and the earliest messianic communities. In the life and ministry of Jesus he finds the governing principle for Christian ministry. "The nucleus of the whole of this ministry is the God of human beings, concerned for humanity, who wants to make us people of God, in turn, like God, concerned for other people" (p. 24). Jesus' actions signaling the inbreaking of the kingdom reveal God's stance with regard to human beings. With a special concern for the poor, Jesus proclaims that the kingdom is "a new world in which suffering is done away with, a world of completely whole or healed people in a society no longer dominated by master-servant relationships" (p. 21). Christian ministry must be acting in service of the kingdom as Jesus did. Fundamentally ministry is the praxis of the kingdom of God, which Schillebeeckx defines as "salvation for human beings" (p. 21).

In the earliest Christian missionary communities, which saw themselves as imbued with the Spirit through baptism in the name of Jesus, this concern for humanity was continued. It is Schillebeeckx's claim that these early, pre-Pauline communities were pneumatic and egalitarian. By virtue of the gift of the Spirit each person had authority in the community according to his or her own charism. There was leadership and some structure in the community, but this was on the basis of the gift of the Spirit from which no one was excluded in principle. Galatians 3:26–28, which was probably used as part of a baptismal liturgy, epitomizes this earliest tradition. This text stands as a continuing challenge to the Christian community as it evaluates its ministry.

Very early on in the missionary development of the church it became necessary to make decisions about how the church would live its life in very different social and cultural circumstances. Certain adaptions were made for reasons of what Schillebeeckx calls "pastoral strategy." In the interests of the good of the Christian mission, for example, Paul advocates some accommodation to the Greco-Roman society in which Christians will have to live.

This involves a certain weakening of the uncompromising egalitarianism of Galations. Without judging Paul's action, Schillebeeckx points out that this was a pastoral choice from among a number of options and within a certain social cultural situation. It sets a precedent for Christian communities continuing to make pastoral adaptations when confronted with new social and cultural situations. The particular choices Paul and the earliest Christians made are not binding norms, but the need to make such choices for the good of the gospel *is* such a norm.

For Schillebeeckx, this earliest period in the church's history is enormously significant. As he follows the growth and development of the church's ministry he sees this pattern of pastoral adaptation repeated. What should be remembered from these very early days of the church is that ministry essentially is in service of the message of Jesus, which was one of concern and liberation for all humanity. Ministry is carried on in a community in which *all* are empowered with the authority of the Spirit. Ministry goes wrong when the liberating message of the gospel is obscured by stratified ministerial structures that make particular legitimate choices divinely normative for all time and when the fundamental fact of the Spirit-filled nature of the *whole* community is forgotten.

As the practice and theology of ministry evolved beyond the earliest communities, Schillebeeckx notes a tendency toward more institutionalization and uniformity in structure. This is characteristic of groups as they move beyond their foundation period and begin to face conflict situations. Conflicts eventually lead to the question of the locus of authority to resolve such disputes. There begins to grow up in the early church a more uniform differentiation of ministries, an incipient church order, although with a good deal of variety remaining.

Ephesians 4:11 lists apostles, prophets, evangelists, pastors, and teachers as those whose services are consistently necessary for the building up of the community. It is generally agreed that the ministry of apostle, listed first and regarded as the highest authority, did not continue beyond this first constitutive phase of the Christian community. In the Pauline understanding, the apostle was a supralocal leader whose authority was connected to missionary activity. Paul himself is the premier example of the role of the apostle. His letters and many missionary journeys express a constant concern for and oversight of the communities he had founded. In this foundational period, the "more-than-local" leadership of the apostle was exercised alongside the other ministries named in Ephesians that served the local life of the community.

As is normal also in the organization of groups the early Christians tended to adopt forms of organization familiar to them either from their civic life in the Greco-Roman world or from their Jewish past. This led to some diversity in organization in the early communities and eventually to a merging of these patterns of organization. This resulted in the consolidation and strengthening of the local leadership in the persons of the presbyter-bishops, presbyter, and deacons. With the death of the apostles and the advent of heretical groups claiming to have the true doctrine of Jesus, the question of doctrinal authority in the community arose with even more urgency. By the time of the later New Testament this authority was appropriated by the local leadership, albeit still with much fluidity in its exercise. By the time of Clement, this tripartite structure is seen as divinely intended and theologically legitimated. With this theology, Schillebeeckx says, a system of authority and subjection becomes theologically and christologically legitimated and the authority and the many ministries exercised by the Spirit-filled community ultimately become subsumed into the one ministry and authority of the bishop.

Certain historical and sociological choices thus led to a particular church structure. What was the theological significance of such choices? In a survey of New Testament texts Schillebeeckx identifies a number of theological concerns related to these choices: first, a concern for the preservation of the apostolic tradition in the postapostolic community; second, a developing understanding of the meaning of leadership in a Christian community; and third, recognition of certain characteristics that might be demanded of one who exercises such leadership (pp. 92–93). These issues color the presentation of ministry in the Matthean, Marcan, Lucan and Johannine traditions reported in these gospels as well as in the post-Pauline Letter to the Ephesians. They indicate that the development toward institutionalization during this New Testament period was seen as necessary for the survival and continued growth of the community in what were often considered to be hostile surroundings. In response to changing circumstances, certain of the ministries emerged as more permanent and stable functions in the community. In Ephesians, for example, proclamation, leadership, and building up the community are noted as central ministerial functions. Leadership is one among many necessary services. How people are appointed to these tasks, however, does not yet appear as a matter of concern. What *is* a concern is continuing fidelity to the community's apostolic origins. These tasks are in service to that goal.

It is important to mention Schillebeeckx's understanding of apostolicity, since his interpretation of apostolic succession, which has been a matter of some discussion, is grounded in this notion. In its earliest connotation apostolicity characterized the self-understanding of the *whole* community conscious of its roots in the apostolic proclamation of the gospel of Jesus Christ. By the time of the Pastoral epistles apostolicity is more closely connected to the ministry of leadership in the community. This is connected, however, not with any concern for a *certain* structure or for a mechanical or physical notion of succession but rather with the central concern of the Pastorals for continuity or succession in authentic teaching. Thus the particular structure that has evolved by the time of the Pastorals is not normative, but rather their linkage of ministry with a concern for authentic doctrine. Laying on of hands, Schillebeeckx suggests, arose in the church as a way to ensure the permanent presence of ministry in the church as well as a sign of that presence.

In response to criticism of his understanding of apostolic succession Schillebeeckx outlines what he calls "four dimensions of apostolicity": (1) the churches are built on the apostles and prophets; (2) the apostolic tradition, of which the New Testament writings are a permanent foundation document; (3) the apostolicity of the whole community, which is signified by doing as Jesus did in his ministry; and (4) the apostolicity of church ministries that became known as apostolic succession (p. 116). For Schillebeeckx, *all* of these elements in relationship to one another are important in the characterization of the Christian community as apostolic. "Ministry is important but it is only one of many authorities which are concerned to preserve and keep alive and intact the gospel of Jesus Christ" (p. 117). The leadership ministry in the church is in service of the wider apostolicity of the whole community.

Within the general evolution toward more centralized structures, Schillebeeckx notes some countervailing trends. Both the Johannine and Marcan traditions, while accepting the need for some structure and authority, relativize these in face of the conviction of the continued presence of the risen Jesus through the indwelling of the Spirit. The Matthean tradition also witnesses to an earlier more charismatic exercise of authority and a suspicion toward office bearers. Schillebeeckx points out, however, a certain cautionary note in the early disappearance of communities that never made the pastoral accommodation of a certain institutionalizing of ministry. Some institutionalization is necessary for survival over the long term. The general experience of these early communities points to the ongoing tension that remains with us today between the charism of all the believers and the "institutionalized limitation of this same charisma" (p. 92).

Also worth retrieving for today's discussions of ministry are certain essential characteristics of ministry and ministers that Schillebeeckx discovers in the testimonies of these early communities. In the Marcan corpus particularly he finds a distinctive Christian reinterpretation of the exercise of power and authority. "Pagan leadership is based on power and ruling with an iron fist, but Christian leadership of a community must be service: ministers must be slaves, serve (10:42–44), as did Jesus (10:45)" (p. 87). This theme is of course also underlined in John in the foot-washing account.

In Luke Schillebeeckx also sees some qualities that illumine the meaning of Christian ministry. The service of the minister is bearing witness to the gospel. The minister must devote him- or herself to Jesus' cause continued in the life of the community. This will involve suffering and even death in some cases. Those who have been tested by suffering are thus candidates for the ministry. But suffering is not the whole picture; the minister is also one who should contribute to the joy of the community by proclaiming the message of liberation and reconciliation (p. 93).

Finally, Schillebeeckx's investigation of the New Testament data points out that ministry did not in the first instance develop exclusively in relation to the Eucharist. One presided at the Eucharist in virtue of one's leadership of the community. Leadership was a charism that was called forth by the community for the service of the community. It thus would have been an anomaly in this earliest period of the church's history to have a community without Eucharist or authorized leaders.

THE ASSESSMENT OF DEVELOPMENT: CONTINUITY AND CHANGE

The witness of the New Testament clearly has particularly normative and illuminative possibilities for ministry today in Schillebeeckx's view. He does, however, particularly in *The Church with a Human Face*, look seriously at post–New Testament developments in the structure and spirituality of ministry for both positive and negative trends. In his view today's situation must be confronted with the lessons of the whole tradition of ministry.

In the progress of history, for complex sociological as well as theological reasons, Schillebeeckx discerns a progressive narrowing of the rich understanding of ministry described in the pages of the New Testament. This narrowing began with certain directions already obvious, although not central, as early as the second century and maybe earlier. Although there was a good deal of diversity among the various local churches in the first centuries, one can discern a gradual movement toward an increased focusing of the ministerial charisms given to all through baptism on the specific ministries of the bishops, presbyters (who eventually became identified as priests), and deacons, gradually focusing centrally on the bishop and ultimately the pope. Understandings of these ministerial roles changed and developed as the church became increasingly institutionalized, often taking on the civil structures of a particular culture or period. During these first centuries also the liturgical rite of ordination, connected to laying on of hands, became more central, at first as a recognition of the call and missioning of the community that was considered to be the essential element of ordination.

In addition to the progressive hierarchialization of ministry Schillebeeckx sees in these early centuries, he also notes an initial sacerdotalization of ministry. Two particular developments are central to this process. The advent by the fourth century of "country priests," presbyters who went out from the great urban centers of Christianity to celebrate the Eucharist for rural communities, led to viewing these presbyters as "priests" whose functions were increasingly identified in relationship to the Eucharist. Second, the fourth-century declaration of Christianity as the state religion fostered the interpretation of Christianity as a cultic community analogous to previous imperial religions. "As a result the priesthood itself was connected one-sidedly with the Eucharist as the highpoint of the cult" (p. 143). Schillebeeckx sees this development as a significant break with the New Testament understanding. That the link between the Eucharist and community leadership was not entirely broken during this period is attested to by the prohibition of the sixth canon of the Council of Chalcedon against absolute ordinations.

By the early Middle Ages a hierarchical, cultic understanding of the ministry was widespread. A pyramidal image of the church dominated, with the hierarchy at the top. A laity who were the passive recipients of their ministry formed the base. An increasingly sacrificial interpretation of the Eucharist reinforced the cultic identification of the priesthood.

It is Schillebeeckx's contention that these clericalizing, hierarchializing, sacerdotalizing trends came to dominate the understanding of priesthood over the next centuries, eventually leading to what he calls the classical modern notion of the priest, which was legitimated, although not born, at the Council of Trent. This of course was not a unilateral development and Schillebeeckx notes countervailing trends in the variety of images of the priest that have appeared through history.

Of particular importance to Schillebeeckx's thesis is the increasing tendency one finds from the eighth to the thirteenth century to identify ordination exclusively in relation to the cult of the Eucharist and to separate this from jurisdiction that related to pastoral responsibility for a community. The great monastic orders had many priests with no pastoral charge. This reality as well as the rise of the mendicant orders, which saw their tasks as supraterritorial, contributed to the split between ordination and jurisdiction. New conceptions of law reinforced this separation. An ordained man possessed personally the priestly power to confect the Eucharist even though he might not be assigned to any Christian community and thus did not have the power of jurisdiction. "If a man has been personally ordained priest, he has the 'power of the Eucharist' and can therefore celebrate it on his own. For the early church this was inconceivable" (p. 193).

For Schillebeeckx, this split between ordination and jurisdiction, characteristic of second-millennium Christianity, is a second significant break in the history of ministry. Priesthood more and more was viewed as a personal state of life than as service to the community; a priest was a higher-status Christian in a world where everyone was baptized. Priests became sacral persons. More emphasis was placed on the ritual as the locus of the conferral of the power of ordination (absolute ordination) even without specific reference to service to a particular Christian community. The priest was ordained more to confect the eucharistic body of Christ than to preside over the ecclesial body of Christ.

An example of the consequences of this split between ordination and jurisdiction with significance for today is the medieval debate over lay preaching. The question was whether preaching was related to jurisdiction, i.e., whether it was a function of leadership in the community or whether it related to ordination, thus giving it a sacramental base in the consecration to priesthood. Twelfth-century theology rooted preaching in ordination. The thirteenth-century solution was that the *missio canonica*, which granted jurisdiction, conferred the authority to preach. Theoretically this latter decision might have opened the door to lay preaching but the hierarchical climate of the time led to a prohibition against such and the reservation of preaching to the clergy.

Schillebeeckx illustrates the relevance of these medieval debates by inserting in this context his reflection on a similar contemporary discussion. Lay preaching is once again a major issue in the church. The new code of canon law roots an implicit acceptance of lay preaching in the necessity of the church to grant jurisdiction to the nonordained for many ministerial functions where there is a shortage of priests. This maintains a separation of ordination and jurisdiction and is hard to reconcile with the Vatican II assertion that the power of ordination is the sacramental basis of jurisdictional authority. Schillebeeckx suggests that this apparent discrepancy points to a perhaps unintentional implication in the new code that the sacramental foundation of both jurisdiction and ordination is to be found in the common baptism of all Christians. This has important consequences for evaluating the increasing involvement of the nonordained in many aspects of leadership and pastoral care in the church. Such activity can be clearly evaluated as truly sacramental and ministerial. From this detour into the present Schillebeeckx returns to his historical journey.

THE "MODERN" PRIEST

The trends Schillebeeckx traces through history as "legitimate although not necessary" responses to various social and theological situations eventually culminated in what he calls the modern or classical understanding of the priest. Starting with the period just prior to the Council of Trent (1545–1563) he sees solidified a clear though unintentional break with the earliest understandings of ministry. The council fathers, in attempting to remain in continuity with what they saw as the constant tradition of the church, served to canonize and make central the narrowing cultic trends the gradual development of which Schillebeeckx traces through the church's history. His contention is that there has resulted from this gradual development a significant difference between early first-millennium and late second-millennium interpretations of Christian ministry.

Hermeneutical studies of Trent have pointed out the complexity of this council and the necessity of understanding its historical context as well as the need to probe the intentions of the fathers behind the texts. Schillebeeckx points out, however, that in fact our modern understanding of the priest has been influenced by the texts themselves and how they were received and transmitted. What has been characterized as the "Tridentine view" has been the central understanding of the priesthood to the present. This view reinforced the split between ordination and jurisdiction and solidified the tendency to identify priesthood one-sidedly with cultic activity, consecration, and absolution. This narrowed priestly image led to the problematic assumption mentioned above, that Christ was a priest on the basis of his divinity rather than his humanity and that priests are personally, mystically elevated above other baptized believers through their identification

THE PRAXIS OF THE KINGDOM OF GOD / 129

with Christ. This became a popular understanding of the meaning of the "character" associated with ordination. Thomas Aquinas, on the contrary, understands character to relate to the call and acceptance by the community for church service. The Council of Trent, although mentioning the character attached to priesthood, does not define the term.

Vatican II made some attempts to rethink the theological foundations of ministry. As mentioned above, it grounds jurisdiction sacramentally in ordination. It more often describes ministry as service than as power and it does recognize the common baptism of all the believers as the essential root of all ministry. But despite its ecclesiological emphasis it does not completely separate itself from the direct christological approach to ordained ministry that Schillebeeckx sees as a source of contemporary problems.

Thus, at the end of his historical investigation, Schillebeeckx returns to the issue that is the leitmotif of his ministerial thinking. Ministry cannot be understood apart from community and there can be no community without ministry. This connection has been obscured in modern understandings of priesthood and must be restored if the present-day crisis in ministry is to be resolved. The present-day situation in which there are communities deprived of ordained ministers and thus of the Eucharist would be an anomaly if the proper relationship between the christological and the ecclesiological were to be understood. Because the church is the place where the Spirit dwells, "the church itself is the womb of the ministry, which is itself in the service of the community of believers " (p. 207).

There are in fact sufficient leaders in the Christian community today, but because of present structures growing out of contingent historical choices, such as mandatory celibacy and the exclusion of women, many of these leaders are unable to preside at the Eucharist. It is Schillebeeckx's conviction that once again, as history illustrates has happened many times before, the understanding of ministry must adapt to changing needs. Antecedent to any existing structures, the Christian community has a right to leaders and to the Eucharist. If the important connection between ministry and service to the community were restored, it would be clear that those persons, male or female, who are called to the service of leadership by the Spirit-filled community should in virtue of that role preside at the community Eucharist. This leadership should be recognized by appropriate ritual and communication, and mutual critique with other Christian communities should be fostered.

It should be made clear that Schillebeeckx nowhere in his works on ministry defends the idea that "laypersons" should preside at the Eucharist. He in fact cites instances of this as among the negative experiences that prompt his reflections. He states clearly and unambiguously that his consistent position has been that "those faithful who in fact lead and animate a Christian community, such as 'lay ministers,' must be given an appropriate ecclesial recognition, and therefore the laying on of hands" (*Tijdschrift voor Theologie* 25 (1985): 180–81, Trans. R. J. Schreiter).

Beyond this general principle Schillebeeckx does not offer universal suggestions for a more appropriate practice of ministry. It is his conviction that a new theology of ministry must be arrived at "from below," from reflection on the concrete praxis of diverse, pluralistic Christian communities brought into mutually critical dialogue with Scripture and Christian history. The gospel understanding of ministry as active involvement in the cause of Jesus Christ as well as the gospel characteristics of freedom, liberation, and joy should serve as evaluative criteria for the authenticity of contemporary praxis. In critical reflection on present-day experience, illumined by the lessons of the past, the Christian community will discover a practice and theology of ministry that will allow the church to be experienced as the human face of God for our time.

SUGGESTIONS FOR FURTHER READING

The fullest and most recent presentation of Schillebeeckx's thought on ministry may be found in *The Church with a Human Face*. For a briefer and earlier discussion see "The Christian Community and its Office Bearers," in *The Right of a Community to a Priest, Concilium* 133 (New York: Seabury, 1980), pp. 95–133. An interesting dialogue highlighting the role of critical communities may be found in "Critical Communities and Office in the Church," in *God Is New Each Moment*, pp. 79–90.

9. A Prophetic Vision: Eschatology and Ethics

BRADFORD E. HINZE

There is a time to be born and a time to die. There is a time for conversion and a time for commitment, a time for the stability of tradition and a time for criticism. There is a time for conflict and a time for reconciliation, a time for political action and a time for prayer. There is a time for every season under heaven.

Eschatology is about living within time. It is about the many dimensions of our temporal existence: our sense of direction and what threatens and inspires our journey into the future. Our perspective on time can be distorted by the rut of routine, by cynicism and despair, and by the denial of our own finitude and death. We may grow stagnant and nostalgic, or become restless and filled with a sense of apocalyptic doom. Whatever temporal moods and attitudes may dominate our individual and communal lives they influence many things—how we view continuity and change, how we view prayer and political action, how we look at birth and death, sin and grace, and God's relation to human history.

Christian eschatology reflects on the tensions and fulfillment of time and history. Where do we find the presence and absence of God in the drama of our life, the life of our community, and the history of the world? Through sacrament and prayer the Christian life in the present is shaped and guided by our memories of the past. Yet we are not to repeat this past; instead we are called continually into an unknown future. Our hope in God, the future of the human race, is rooted in a prayerful solidarity with all those who search for fullness of life and ethical resolve in a world marred by sin, pain, and grief.

Eschatology has been a constant concern for Edward Schillebeeckx. There has been however, a most profound transition in his thinking about this subject. His earliest work (before 1967) contends that history must be understood in light of the mystery of the incarnation of Christ as "the sacrament of the encounter with God." Schillebeeckx's later work continues to affirm the early claim about Jesus as sacrament, but it is placed in a tensive and productive relationship to his growing conviction that history must be understood in relation to Jesus Christ as the decisive "eschatological prophet." As we shall explore, Schillebeeckx creatively combines these two themes in his eschatology, and this eschatology provides the framework for understanding his contribution to ethics and the appropriation of liberation theology.

EARLY SACRAMENTAL ESCHATOLOGY

Early in his career Schillebeeckx employed the resources of phenomenology and personalism to reinterpret the dominant and classic vision of history bequeathed to the church by Augustine and reiterated by Thomas Aquinas. Following in this tradition, Schillebeeckx points out that since we are embodied spirits who learn through our senses and we are personal beings, we encounter this invisible God most clearly through Jesus Christ, the Word made flesh. The incarnate one is the decisive revelation of God to the human community, the source of reconciliation, and the perfect model of the worship of God through prayer and actions. The meaning of history is disclosed through this human encounter with Jesus Christ.

With his death, Jesus is no longer present as the physical mediator. This void is filled by the church, which becomes in history the earthly extension of the body of the risen Lord. History from the death of Christ to the parousia is all of one kind, the age of the church. It is through the church that Christ is mystically encountered and within this community worshiped and served.

Schillebeeckx has clearly shown to a new generation why this sacramental eschatology remains the dominant model within Christian theology. It provides a theological rationale for the saving presence of Christ and for the church's mission. A wide variety of issues about christology, soteriology, ecclesiology, and about the mystical and ethical dimensions of Christianity are treated with impressive coherence and adequacy to human experience. Through Christ the created order, which has been frustrated by sin, is brought to fulfillment. The experience of Christ's grace within the Christian community is the basis of our hope for eternal life in God.

This model of eschatology strongly affirms the importance of historical mediation—the making present of an invisible God through physical, human, and institutional forms, as well as the necessary mediation of the religious message down through history with the aid of philosophical and other nontheological languages and insights. Moreover, a sacramental eschatology enables the church to acknowledge ambiguity and ambivalence within history; ambiguity, because the mediation of God does take place outside of Christianity through the so-called sacraments of nature, history, and historical religions, even though they pale in comparison to the primary sacrament, Christ (*Christ the Sacrament*, pp. 7–13); and ambivalence, because ethical purity is not the prerequisite for participation in the Christian community and the practical decisions Christians make are seldom made with apodictic certainty.

A PROPHETIC REFORMULATION

Schillebeeckx in his later work has identified several deficiencies in the sacramental model of eschatology, while continuing to affirm its basic tenets about mediation, ambiguity, and ambivalence. A sacramental eschatology proves susceptible to criticism on two fronts. First, recent historical-critical study of the Scriptures clearly shows that prophetic and apocalyptic eschatologies are present in the Jewish milieu in which the person and mission of Jesus must be understood. Second, liberation theologians, Latin American, black, and feminist theologians among others, point out that the scandal of massive human suffering and oppression poses a religious question in need of response. What both of these recent developments have in common is that, more than the sacramental approach, they focus on moments of crisis in history that call forth the divine judgment and vindication. The prophetic eschatology at work in the earliest New Testament testimony and in present-day communities of liberation fights against incipient dualistic, pietistic, otherworldly interpretations of history.

Rather than speak about a history divided into the city of human-kind and the city of God, a natural plane and a supernatural plane, or a secular history and a sacred history, there is an insistence upon the oneness of history (*Christ*, p. 561).

In his historical-critical study of the New Testament Schillebeeckx attempts to uncover "the human face of God" in Jesus. However, in the *Jesus* volume, this sacramental mediation is now transformed by a truly prophetic vision of history. Jesus has prophetic solidarity with the suffering and sinners, because the cause of God is intent on humanity and God does not will suffering. What Schillebeeckx discovers through historical reconstruction of the experience of New Testament Christianity, he also finds displayed in the narrative configuration of the testimony of the Christian community: the Christian community encounters Jesus as a prophet and more than a prophet. It is through this recollection that the church discovers again and again what it means to affirm that Jesus Christ is the Lord of history.

JESUS, THE ESCHATOLOGICAL PROPHET

That we find in Jesus' vision a prophetic and not an apocalyptic eschatology is very important for Schillebeeckx. There are clear indications of a prophetic quality in Jesus' teaching, ministry, and way of life. By bearing in his person the cries of the poor, the sick, and the suffering and voicing the judgment of God against injustice and for human wholeness, Jesus stands clearly within the prophetic tradition that stretches from Moses, down through the prophets Elijah, Amos, Hosea, Jeremiah, and Isaiah. In the face of historical tumult, *apocalyptic* eschatology, by contrast, accents the radical discontinuity between this age and the age to come; it stresses the stern divine judgment upon the human project. Even though Jesus shares certain convictions with apocalyptic eschatology—especially its sense of crisis and divine judgments—he clearly rejects the two-aeons doctrine and the severity of the justice of God upon the human situation in condemning the evil of this age (*Jesus*, pp. 148-54). Rather, in the face of this crisis and judgment, Jesus embodies the promise of God's graciousness and steadfast concern for human wholeness, a stance that requires the rejection of any dualistic vision of history or humanity.

At the heart of the New Testament narrative is Jesus' understanding of himself as the eschatological prophet. In the tradition of Moses and the prophets of Israel he does good in the face of evil and suffering and sides with the marginalized, the sinners, and the suffering. His preaching announces the reign of God, which is God's intent for humanity, and insists that people look to the future and prepare for the full presence of God's reign. When Jesus is faced with the rejection of his message and mode of life and his own possible death, the persecution and martyrdom of Israel's prophets provide him with an interpretive key. Jesus freely accepts the outcome of his life. The resurrection event precipitates the conversion of Jesus' followers and their constitution as a community. In this conversion event God vindicates Jesus' life and ministry and engenders a salvific interpretation of Jesus' life and death.

One of the lasting contributions of Schillebeeckx's christology is that it introduces prophecy as a central category in a sacramental eschatology. The dominant tradition of christology has been framed in terms of a sacramental eschatology. The councils of Nicaea and Chalcedon proclaim the church's judgment about the definitive mediation of salvation through Christ. Schillebeeckx agrees that we dare not reject this tradition. However, he insists that we recognize the earlier, prophetic tradition as the fundamental source of all christological claims. The earliest prophetic Christology stresses that Jesus is the one who brings the approaching salvation. He is the Lord of the future and judge of the world, who recognizes the crisis of suffering in the world and the need for a fundamental change of vision. This christology ought to remain in a creative if tensive relationship with the later sacramental formulations. Seen from this marriage of viewpoints, Christ remains the sacrament of the encounter with God within history, but this claim is no longer tied to an understanding of time since Christ as unchanging and unthreatened.

JESUS, THE NEW HUMANITY, AND SALVATION

The prophetic modification of the sacramental eschatology likewise transforms our understanding of soteriology and ethics. Christological formulations originate in Jesus' question, "Who do you say that I am?" But this question about Jesus always includes a question about ourselves: "What is the saving significance of Jesus for me as an individual and for us as a community?" Traditionally this is spoken of as the inseparable relationship between the person of Christ and the work of Christ. Christological claims have always been guided by their soteriological impact (*Jesus*, pp. 564–656; *Christ*).

In Schillebeeckx's mature formulation, the mystery of Jesus Christ continues to serve as the primal point of mediation for salvation. However, Jesus' mission is no longer spoken of in Thomistic terms as "a mystery of saving worship: a mystery of praise (the upward movement) and of salvation (the downward movement)," or as "the divine love for humans and the human love for God: bestowal of grace and religious worship." (*Christ the Sacrament*, pp. 17–20). Instead, Jesus' mediation is now imbued with a prophetic force: as the definitive eschatological prophet, Jesus is the parable of God and the paradigm of humanity (*Jesus*, pp. 626ff.). Jesus in his message and praxis "identifies himself in person with the cause of God as that also of humans (God's rule, which people have to seek first, before everything else), and with the cause of human beings as God's cause (the kingdom of God as a kingdom of peace and salvation among people (*Jesus*, p. 269). The transition is not simply from a worship-centered vision of salvation to an action-centered one, although the accent lies there. More importantly there is a preconception of salvation that leaves behind the theory of the supernatural with its two-tiered view of history.

Jesus is the *parable of God* by showing God's concern for human wholeness. In every period in history humans crave "wholeness" (*Jesus*, pp. 153, 621; *Christ*, pp. 62–64). Jesus in the New Testament has solidarity with all those who hunger for wholeness, who are torn apart by the contrast experiences of sin, suffering, and oppression. Those who encounter Jesus have experienced God's absence and the negative sacraments of exclusion and pain. These people cry aloud or in silent tears for God's divine compassion and judgment. Here people experience the hiddenness of God and long for the sacramental presence through body, touch, and commitment.

This longing for human wholeness that springs so vividly from the pages of the New Testament is ultimately the longing for salvation. But what constitutes human wholeness—what is meant by salvation—is articulated differently in different epochs; eternal life beyond death; freedom from internal bondage, sin, and guilt; courage in facing the anxiety of finitude. With this ongoing reconceptualization, the church's understanding of salvation has been deepened, broadened, and made more precise. In our own day the social character and effects of sin are recognized in patterns of economic, racial, and sexual injustice perpetuated by institutions, social structures, traditions, and customs. Accordingly, redemption must be clarified in relation to the human longing for wholeness and release from oppression and suffering. Redemption includes the quest for human liberation as a manifestation of God's intent for humanity.

Jesus is the *paradigm for humanity.* His actions and person not only show God's concern for humanity; they also provide a model for our lives. Salvation is disclosed in the gracious working of the kingdom in our midst through conversion, as a gift and task. "Jesus makes a connection between a coming of God's rule and *metanoia,* that is, the actual praxis of the kingdom of God. ... This connection between God's lordship and orthopraxis clearly derives from Jesus: in his 'going about, doing good,' in his taking sides with the dispossessed and outcast, which comes out especially in his parables and his associating with sinners. ... Orthopraxis, right conduct, is the human manifestation or logical rendering of God's universal saving love, registered in practical human living" (*Jesus,* p. 153).

Christ is the parable of God and the paradigm of humanity, for through him we are freed from the powers of sin, death, and oppression, which shackle the self in vital, personal, and social ways, and we are freed for ethical action in the world as an anticipation and furthering of the kingdom of God. "Liberation from various forms of human slavery and the fear of death is both the consequence of the adoption of grace or birth from God and also the requirement of grace. ... Liberation is not only liberation from unjust conditions for something good; what persons are freed for is itself a command to free humans from unjust circumstances, for it is redemption within a world which is still damaged and sick. All this indicates that redemption and liberation in the New Testament are both a gift and a task to be realized" (*Christ,* p. 513).

Schillebeeckx's shift to a prophetically oriented sacramental eschatology moves Christianity's center of gravity from the past or present to the future. Mediation still remains central, as we shall explore in more detail, but it is not mediation grounded in the theory of participation so crucial for Greek and Latin thought in early Christian theology and a lasting theme through the work of Thomas Aquinas. Nor is mediation any longer rooted in a doctrine of creation understood as the divine disclosure of an unchanging order in cosmos and human nature. Rather we are left only with an anticipation of a total meaning and with a patient hope and trust in the God of Jesus Christ (*Jesus*, p. 618). This means that the universal meaning and unity of history is not grounded in an understanding of the divine providence of God that affirms a preordained plan based on the being and order of nature and cosmos. Instead, since "the question of universal meaning (in history) *qua* question is given inevitably," then it may be affirmed that "history is only potentially one" (*Jesus*, p. 615).

The unity of history is not reducible to the significance of the human subject, just as theology and ethics are not reducible to anthropology. Schillebeeckx continues to maintain that God remains the subject and the universal meaning of history, even if this is only understood in fragments now. The God of Jesus Christ is the Lord of history. While salvation as human wholeness may be the guiding theme within this history, the quest for wholeness cannot be reduced to personal piety, ethical action, or sociopolitical involvement (*Christ*, p. 717).

ETHICS

Important ethical ramifications follow from Schillebeeckx's dynamic sacramental and prophetic construal of history, Christ, and salvation. It is no longer possible to find a secure ethical foundation in any objectivistic construal of human nature or natural law. Instead the Christian finds socially and historically conditioned ethical models at work in the New Testament and throughout the history of Christianity that mediate Christian conversion to praxis. These concrete models are essential for understanding the ethical character of Christianity, but they can never provide "a *direct* answer to ethical questions which are posed in terms of a different cultural model" (*Christ*, p. 593).

Schillebeeckx concludes that the New Testament has no specific ethical principle, no ethic of the categorical imperative, no commandments or prohibitions, no virtues or values that are not socially and historically conditioned. Any attempt to make the concrete ethical models of the Bible into lasting determinate norms is susceptible to criticism. So, for instance, Paul's statements about the subordination of women, slaves, and citizens to their sexual, racial, and social or economic superiors cannot be viewed as transhistorically binding. Nor are his statements against divorce and in favor of virginity sacrosanct. Such models offer prototypes of ethical behavior, not archetypes. To grant these models transhistorical validity is hermeneutically misguided, since it ignores the social and historical location in which those ethical claims were made and tends to accord norms absolute validity by way of an undialectical sacramental notion of history (*Christ*, pp. 586–600).

An important problem poses itself here: since we have denied that there is any clear moral objectivity rooted in a created order and a natural law and have affirmed the historically and socially conditioned character of ethical judgments within the Bible and throughout Christianity, are we left with a radical moral relativism? There are several levels of response to this question.

It must first be recognized that everyone discerns ethical norms and is ethically motivated through historical models and communal narratives (*Christ*, pp. 655, 658). This is true not only for Christians, but for Buddhists, Sikhs, Moslems, humanists, and all other religious and historical traditions. A radically autonomous interpretation of the self rejects the mediation of ethical values and norms through traditions and communities and consequently fails to understand the historical character of a community's ethos. Simply stated, there is no point outside of history for addressing ethical questions and adjudicating ethical conflicts.

The biblical ethic does not offer Christians any eternal moral sureties, but at the center of this testimony there is the conviction that "the New Testament will not separate ethics from religion"

(*Christ*, p. 590). Though ethical discourse can take place outside of the sphere of religious discourse, for Christians the religious quest and the ethical impulse are irrevocably fused. The mystical dimension of Christianity taps our human receptivity to the givenness and gift of reality. Mystical experience establishes a relationship to the reality of God, which grounds our meaningful and truthful discourse about the God of Jesus Christ and orients us to a way of being and acting in accordance with the divine reality.

The mystical encounter brought about through Christian conversion yields an ethical life-style and commitment. An ethical way of life is logically distinct yet inseparable from religion, especially within Christianity. "Ethics has a certain independence, but the believer or the religious person sees its deepest foundation, source, and ground in the reality of God" (*Christ*, p. 59). And in turn, "the religious manifests itself in the ethical, and as a result transforms the merely 'natural' significance of ethics" (*Christ*, p. 599).

The Christian transformation of ethical discourse is tied to the twofold claim that "Christian ethics has a christological and eschatological foundation" (*Christ*, p. 600). The christological foundation for Christian ethics is located in the life and teachings of Jesus. Christians are called to a continual *metanoia*, which means that we are called to make "our history, following Jesus" (*Christ*, p. 641). What this entails is only ascertainable by examining the prophetic quality of Jesus, presented in the gospel narratives through his teaching in parables about the kingdom of God and most clearly manifest in the beatitudes and in his solidarity with the suffering and marginalized. Jesus's life is to be imitated, but this must be reinterpreted into our own day and age. The traditional distinction between counsel and precept wrongly spiritualizes the meaning of the beatitudes and disintegrates their potency. However, neither are the beatitudes for legal codification. Rather, Jesus' words and actions in solidarity with the marginalized constitute a utopian critical force that evokes an ethical conversion and a commitment to the ethical task on behalf of the constantly threatened *humanum*. This is the metaphoric power of the parable, the symbolic force of the paradigm. Jesus reveals what is and what can be.

The eschatological foundation for Christian ethics is determined by the tensive relationships between the church and the world and between the kingdom of God and human history. The sacramental and prophetic character of this tension is embodied in word and deed by Jesus. The sacramental eschatology affirms the presence and power of God in the world and the church through creation and grace, but this model risks dissolving the ambiguity and ambivalence in history by legitimating a "logic of triumph." Such a triumphalism has at times led the church to support an alliance between the ecclesial and secular authorities or values, failing to call into question the finitude and sinfulness of either the church or the world. The later Schillebeeckx certainly acknowledges the real, if fragmentary mediation of God in creation and grace through the church for the wholeness of the human race. Yet this is now tempered by the prophetic awareness that the "reign of God," though truly anticipated in the church and the world, will be fully manifest only in the end. What results is a nuanced recognition of the ways that the eschatological kingdom of God is manifested in the historical gift and task of salvation in the church and the world. "Ethical life . . . is the *recognizable* content of salvation, the historical manifestation or demonstration of the imminence of the kingdom of God. . . . Through its ethical effects the kingdom of God is present in our history in nondefinitive forms which keep on becoming obsolete. Ethical improvement of the world is *not* the kingdom of God (any more than it is the church), but it is an anticipation of that kingdom" (*Christ,* p. 599).

Christians have too often been incapacitated for action in the world, especially political action, by their interpretation of this eschatological proviso. Schillebeeckx joins liberation theologies here in three ways. First, he points out that even the early Christians recognized the need for ethical action and for structural change, even though this was envisioned primarily within the confines of the church (*Christ,* pp. 561-67). Second, as we have seen already, for Schillebeeckx previous concrete ethical models are prototypes, not diachronic norms, instances of "human ethics" tied to certain historical and social conditions, yet reinterpreted by Christianity. Third, while the fullness of redemption and human wholeness is never realized in history, the church's mission is to promote salvation and liberation within history personally, communally, and politically.

An important question remains: what about the ethical discourse that is distinct from and transformed by religious discourse? Schillebeeckx explicitly rejects Thomas Aquinas's natural law method and any other system that would find in nature an eternally binding ethical order. Yet he does stand with Thomas and probably with numerous revised natural law theorists in affirming the "relative independence of ethics on a human basis" (*Christ*, p. 655). Schillebeeckx also differs from the tradition by insisting that there is no decisive disclosure of what the *humanum* is either in creation or historical revelation. As an eschatological concept, the *humanum*—genuine humanity—will be realized only in the future. "The *humanum*, threatened and in fact already damaged, leads specifically and historically to ethical demand and the ethical imperative, and thus to confrontation with quite definite, negative experiences of contrast. Therefore ethical invitation or demand is not an abstract norm, but historically, an event *which presents a challenge:* our concrete history itself, humans in need, humankind in need" (*Christ*, p. 659). "We do not have a preexisting definition of humanity—indeed for Christians it is not only a future, but an eschatological reality" (*Christ*, p. 731).

Schillebeeckx's ethics is clearly based on a conversion to imitate Jesus by conforming to the biblical narrative as kept alive in the memory of the church. He is not concerned with the relationship between narrative and character or with identifying specific virtues in the gospel story. Rather, Schillebeeckx finds in the New Testament narrative a distinctively eschatological ethic. Christian conversion to a mystical and ethical way of life requires searching the possibilities for realizing the as yet unrealized gift of humanity. The gift and task of humanity will be concretely determined differently in each period in history. However, the anchor of the church's ethics, in Schillebeeckx's view, must be the commitment to solidarity with the marginalized and the suffering. The preferential option for the poor provides the biblical basis for a Christian ethics of political responsibility.

The Bible is more than a moral reminder of what we may also discover in the natural or human realm. The eschatological character of Christian witness in the New Testament shakes up our accustomed ways of looking at the world; it disturbs the patterns we have set in our lives: humanity is revealed there as a threatened and unfinished task. Its ongoing power to inspire conversion and commitment makes the utopian prophetic eschatology of the biblical narrative a critical, motivating, and sustaining force within the church and world.

In working out an ethical agenda, Christians must be vigilant. While embracing the sacramental and the prophetic dimensions in an eschatological ethics, Christians must reject utopian extremes on either side. An excessive sacramental eschatology can legitimate a retrospective, conservative utopia that reveres the past as the binding norm and finds only homogeneity in time since Christ. An extreme prophetic vision, one should say apocalyptic on the other hand, can lend itself to a progressive, futuristic utopia that rejects every historical manifestation, ethical, social, religious, and political. Ultimately neither way is able to discern the spirits within history.

More insidious and prevalent in our own day perhaps is a certain kind of rationalistic utopia. Placing their trust in technical rationality, government and business elites make decisions based on efficiency, cost-benefit analysis, and profitability. This utilitarian calculus precludes discussions of the wider public good and the results undercut the ability of those affected to decide their own destinies. The structures of power and the patterns of ownership and distribution too often remain unchallenged. The wheels of economic progress for the few seem regularly primed by the suffering of the oppressed. In Schillebeeckx's view, the practices generated by such rationalistic utopias fall especially under the judgment of the gospel's eschatological vision.

AN ETHICS OF PROPHETIC MEDIATION

Schillebeeckx's prophetic and utopian ethic remains sacramental, requiring the bodily, personal, and institutional mediation of God in Christ and through the church. Jesus Christ mediates salvation as the parable of God and the paradigm of humanity. The Christian church mediates this message within the world. The Christian community mediates salvation to the human race not only by remaining faithful to the work of Christ through prayer, sacraments, and life-style, but also through work for human wholeness and against human bondage. The church fulfills this mission in this mystical ministry of the sacraments and also by being involved in the public debate in the pluralistic society about ethical issues. There is a universalistic intent here, but it is neither absolutistic nor triumphalistic. We enter into the public conversation with the best rational arguments we can provide about the *humanum* on behalf of all who search for human wholeness. While we are motivated by the search for genuine consensus, we realize this is often jeopardized by distortion in language, power dynamics within conversation, and individual or group interest and bias.

The sacramental principle of mediation calls for historical, theoretical, and practical mediations of God's reign through the church's ethical reflection and conversation in the public arena (*On Christian Faith*, pp. 64–65). Schillebeeckx distinguishes three levels of ethical reflection and mediation: anthropological constants, formal norms, and material, concrete moral norms. Ethical values and norms are only learned and mediated through concrete historical models. But while these historical models are indispensable in handing down the ethical impulse, they are not transhistorical. However, "anthropological constants" are disclosed throughout the history of Christianity and other narrative communities that supply a very general system of coordinates. These constants, described more fully in Chapter 5, may be summarized as follows: all persons are corporeal and in nature, intersubjective, and religious; they are conditioned by social and institutional structures, by temporal and spatial determinants; and they work out their destinies through theory and practice.

Formal norms are the "general, dynamic directions which tell us we must promote the *humanum* and not try to slow it down" (*The Schillebeeckx Reader*, p. 261). Formal norms emerge from anthropological constants and are always valid. For example, being just is a formal norm that requires that we promote the values of life, health, social well-being, and so on. Material norms specify formal norms within the relative conditions of history and culture. The abstract—anthropological constants and formal norms—are only discovered through the mediation of concrete moral living. "In contrast to the absolutely valid 'formal norms,' all concrete material norms are therefore relative, historically conditioned, and mutable. Although the formal norm only gains validity concretely in the material norms, which thereby participate in the absolute character of the formal norms, namely, promotion of the *humanum* and the checking and avoiding of all those things which do it damage, these material norms, count only as conditioned" (*The Schillebeeckx Reader*, p. 262).

This principle of ethical mediation finally requires that since there are no transhistorical material norms given in the Bible or in human nature, we need to remain open to insights from philosophical ethics, the natural sciences, and above all the social sciences. The pursuit of economic, racial, and gender justice requires that we learn from social theories in order to understand the social dynamics of continuity and change, harmony and upheaval. And although he severely criticizes technical rationality, Schillebeeckx still insists upon a sober acknowledgement and assessment of the positive human purposes technology may serve.

Christian discipleship requires being both sacramental and prophetic. For Schillebeeckx this means we must live by the eschatological narrative of the gospel, act in solidarity with the suffering and the outcast, and work in hope for the further manifestation of the kingdom in history. Christian faith ultimately entails learning to live with ambiguity and ambivalence within history, for we are ignorant of the future and in the present we find "flashes of light and clouds of impenetrable darkness." There is no blueprint, no cosmic plan in history we can know or follow. The guided memories of Jesus' death and resurrection and our solidarity with those who suffer can shake up our expectations and inspire in us a new work. This remembrance and reunion leads to a mystical surrender to the Lord of history and to an ethical imitation of Jesus as one who does good for those in need.

Within Christian theology there remains a tension between the sacramental and the prophetic approaches to history, just as there is a constant strain between communal stability and the crisis that yields change and between continuity and discontinuity in the church's life. Schillebeeckx neither dissolves these tensions nor offers a haven from the vicissitudes of time. His sacramental and prophetic eschatology requires that practical reason and the discernment of spirits are employed in the concrete efforts at drawing past and present toward God, the hope and future of humanity.

SUGGESTIONS FOR FURTHER READING

For his sacramental interpretation of history see *Christ the Sacrament of the Encounter with God.* This shift to a more prophetic eschatology can be traced, on the one hand, by examining his increasing reference to "negative and contrast experiences" and "the future," beginning with "The Church as the Sacrament of Dialogue," written in 1967 in *God the Future of Man* and, on the other hand, by examining his treatment of Jesus as eschatological prophet as distinct from apocalypticism in the *Jesus* volume. How both the sacramental and prophetic dimensions factor into his vision of salvation and liberation and his view of ethics can be seen in *Christ* and in his *On Christian Faith.* The specifically ethical statements are scattered throughout his work, but can be especially located in *Christ,* Part IV, and *The Schillebeeckx Reader,* pp. 260–71.

10. Edward Schillebeeckx: His Continuing Significance

ROBERT J. SCHREITER, C.PP.S.

The essays in this volume explore a number of different aspects of the multifaceted corpus of Edward Schillebeeckx's theology. No single volume of such reflections could hope to exhaust the many avenues his thought has opened up for a genuinely faithful Christian praxis. And in this concluding section, therefore, no attempt will be made to summarize either his thought or the numerous connections and new prospects the contributors to this volume have suggested. The syntheses and ideas brought forward can stand on their own merit.

What might be more helpful is to return to some of the probings into Schillebeeckx's thought begun by William Hill in his chapter and framed within the sociocultural context of the Low Countries by William Portier in his contribution. In other words, it might be useful to identify some key aspects of Schillebeeckx's thought that account for his continuing attractiveness to such a wide audience, especially in North America.

As both Hill and Portier point out, the attraction to Schillebeeckx does not derive from the symmetries of a carefully crafted system derived from first principles. Schillebeeckx does not share that kind of grand philosophical design with the transcendental Thomists. Nor does it derive from a powerful synthesis of the full range of dogmatic questions. As a number of contributors have pointed out, much of his writing has been incidental, occasioned by pastoral need.

What is it, then, that so fascinates an audience of professional theologians and ordinary believers alike? In his epilogue to *The Schillebeeckx Case*, Ted Schoof notes the outpouring of sentiment at the time of Schillebeeckx's difficulties with the Congregation for the Doctrine of the Faith over his christology books. Many ordinary people wrote to Schillebeeckx, telling him that they had struggled to read those books or that their pastors had "translated" the christology books for them and how much this had meant to them. Is it possible to identify the sources of that attraction?

I would like to suggest that there are four focal points in Schillebeeckx's thought that contribute especially to his long-term significance for Christian theology. While his work is significant for many reasons, it seems to me that these four points tell us something about what it means to do theology at this time in history under the socioeconomic and cultural circumstances of the First World. These four points reveal a series of commitments both to method and to fundamental issues. It is these commitments, then, that have shaped Schillebeeckx's theology since the 1960s and probably need to be attended to by anyone wishing to bring the gospel message into First World realities in the late twentieth century. The four focal points are: a commitment to working inductively; a commitment to the narrative character of experience; a commitment to the mystery of suffering and contrast; and a commitment to the primacy of the soteriological.

WORKING INDUCTIVELY

As was pointed out in the Introduction and in Hill's and Portier's chapters, Schillebeeckx doubts that a great dogmatic system is possible anymore. This sentiment does not grow out of some melancholy about the impossibility of a plausible metaphysics ever undergirding a theological system. Rather, it would seem to represent an intuition into the basic pluralism that marks twentieth-century life and experience. For the gospel message to be heard in such a context of pluralism, it has to be able to touch the immediate and the concrete. It cannot be presumed that there is a common frame of reference. Schillebeeckx's work with critical theory and his awareness of the pervasiveness of human suffering bring with them also a sense of suspicion about frameworks that claim to be comprehensive, for such structures often turn oppressive in order to ensure conformity. His commitment to God's proviso, to the ultimate resolution in the eschatological realm, reflects the fact that all our action and effort cannot be seen as definitive and the fact of how much human suffering is still with us.

This awareness gives his work that searching, tentative character that resonates so immediately with the experience of many who read his work. As Hill points out, Schillebeeckx is concerned with the credibility of Christianity. And by adopting a wayfaring attitude, he can be seen as a guide—one very good guide, but hardly a definitive one—along the road of Christian discipleship today.

So his method represents an inductive, rather than deductive point of departure. "It began with an experience" is a phrase that echoes throughout his christological writings. Even his eclectic use of different methodologies in his theology reflects the need to meet the situation on its own terms rather than force the data into a predetermined form. It is this willingness to confront the issues and the concerns of both the committed Christian and the doubting seeker that has made him so widely read and appreciated.

One phrase of his explored by Janet Callewaert, Donald Goergen, and others in the contributions here is "mediated immediacy." It is Schillebeeckx's attempt to express how finite humans, caught in the vortex of competing claims to knowledge and experience, come to experience the transcendence of God. The pluralism within experience is not all that there is; God and God's grace remain primary. Yet that primacy of grace never manages, in the present age, to erase completely the scars of human suffering. Hence, the quest must continue until the eschatological age is fully upon us. And so there is a continuing need to do theology in an inductive fashion, closely wed to human experience.

THE NARRATIVE CHARACTER OF EXPERIENCE

But does this mean that all we can have to guide us in Christian discipleship are fragments of experience that never come together? Does respect for the plurality of experiences mean that we end up sinking away in a morass of relativism? Schillebeeckx has given considerable thought in recent years to the meaning of experience and how experience relates to Christian revelation and tradition, as Mary Catherine Hilkert points out. Experience can be organized conceptually, but it functions for us most powerfully when threaded together narratively. Concepts focus our experience, but it takes narrative to allow them to express their full range of meaning.

Narrative, however, is not understood naively. Narratives can mislead as well as guide. Hence a critical understanding of narrative is necessary. Schillebeeckx achieves that by reminding us of the subversive narratives of the memory of human suffering, an idea he has taken over from Johannes Baptist Metz. Those "dangerous memories" make us suspect narratives that seem too glib, do not recount the contrast experience of life, and do not portray the struggles toward a fuller *humanum.*

Nor, as Hilkert points out, does Schillebeeckx equate divine revelation with human experience—a danger some theologies dealing with experience do not manage to avoid. For Schillebeeckx, divine revelation falls within human experience, but is not coextensive with it. His growing preoccupation with the prophetic dimension, examined in this book especially by Susan Ross and Bradford Hinze, assures that there will be no facile equation of the two. Revelation comes to us with the narrative of experience and history but always opens us to something beyond that experience and history.

John Galvin captures accurately Schillebeeckx's attempt to see christology as narrative. The subtitle of *Jesus* in the original Dutch edition is "The Story of the Living One." Jesus is indeed "the parable of God," a phrase a number of contributors here have explored. It is not just the drama of the death and resurrection of Jesus that tells us of God, but the entire life and ministry of Jesus, his "praxis of the reign of God." Only by following that narrative can one hope to enter into the parable of God in Jesus Christ. And only by allowing our own narratives to be engaged by that parable can we hope to understand the experience of what God has done for us in Jesus.

Perhaps more than any other theologian, Schillebeeckx has helped restore the narrative of Jesus' life and praxis of the reign of God to this generation of Christians. His work on carefully reconstructing that story has been instrumental in the shift back to the synoptic Gospels away from a sometimes too exclusively Pauline view of the saving work of Jesus. This has certainly been one of the reasons for the widespread interest in his theology. He has helped us engage our stories more intimately with the story of Jesus.

THE MYSTERY OF SUFFERING AND CONTRAST

As Portier points out, Schillebeeckx's focus upon the mystery of suffering and the experience of contrast that that evokes found its expression in his encounter with the work of the early Frankfurt School, especially in the work of Max Horkheimer and Theodor Adorno. And as nearly all the authors in this volume note, that concern with the massiveness of human suffering has become a pervasive theme in all of Schillebeeckx's work since the late 1960s. It has colored deeply his understanding of soteriology, a theme Callewaert explores in considerable detail. It figured into Schillebeeckx's growing interest and involvement with the critical Christian communities (examined here by Susan Ross and Mary Hines) and his more recent interest in liberation theologies (discussed by Hinze).

There are a number of facets to this dimension of Schillebeeckx's thought. Certainly his commitment to concrete, historical experience leaves him little choice but to engage himself with the reality of suffering. But as Goergen points out, Schillebeeckx sees suffering as a mystery and not a problem to be solved by technological rationality or some other means. He sees it in its wrenching depths and realizes that only God can give ultimate relief from it. At the same time, however, the reality of suffering means that any genuine holiness must be a political holiness, a form of sanctity that seeks not only the kingdom within but also forms bonds of solidarity with those who would seek a fuller *humanum*. True holiness has both an ethical dimension and practical consequences for living.

But awe before the mystery of suffering is not the only dimension in Schillebeeckx's understanding of it. He explores in a number of places the revelatory nature of the contrast experiences the encounter with suffering provokes. The contrast opens up not just the opposite of the previously experienced reality, but often new, unexpected worlds as well. Histories that have been suppressed or submerged are allowed to reappear. Many people have come to new understandings of faith and their membership in the church along this pathway. It is often distressing to church leaders, but it is a reality that cannot be denied.

The revelatory nature of contrast experiences raises a third point about Schillebeeckx's use of this idea. There is a profoundly methodological dimension to the utilization of contrast experience. It comes out especially in his discussion of the quest for a universal horizon of meaning toward the end of *Jesus*. One cannot arrive now at a universally agreed upon horizon of meaning that takes into account fully the plurality of legitimate experiences of meaning. One can only engage in a solidarity of struggle to achieve that anticipated horizon. Anticipation finds its place alongside participation as a legitimate mode of experiencing meaning in the world.

By making that assertion, Schillebeeckx introduces an option for a certain asymmetry in his methodology. Deconstructionists especially have pointed out that asymmetry rather than symmetry lies at the basis of experience. Schillebeeckx explores this insight in his own way (and generally more lucidly than do the deconstructionists). The experience of suffering and evil is not simply the symmetrical opposite of experiencing meaning and the good, for if such symmetry were the case, suffering and evil would not be the mystery they are. Nor would pluralism be the reality it is: it would mean that difference is only superficial and ephemeral. For both meaning and nonmeaning to be appreciated in all their fullness they need to be taken seriously in their difference, without one being reduced to the mirror image of the other. To accept symmetry, as the deconstructionists point out, is to accept the hegemony of the status quo imposed by the powerful upon society. Difference needs to be respected.

That insight has grown to be shared by many, especially by feminist thinkers who see how accepting the symmetries of complementarity leads to a return of male domination. Indeed, the experience of asymmetry is considered by many to be a characteristic of the postmodern world. It has long been an experience of oppressed peoples who have seen their worlds of meaning subsumed into a dominant worldview of the powerful. Schillebeeckx's insistence on the contrast experience means that suffering and the encounter with nonmeaning cannot be explained away easily. They must be confronted in all their reality if they are to be overcome ultimately. It is this sense that has given Schillebeeckx's theology a special significance to postmodern people in the First World and to oppressed peoples throughout the entire world who do not see meaning or relief from suffering in places they are told to look.

THE PRIMACY OF THE SOTERIOLOGICAL

What keeps the concentrated focus upon suffering and contrast experiences from fragmenting the praxis of Christian faith? Certainly Schillebeeckx's lifelong insistence on the primacy of God contributes mightily to creating a sense of cohesion in the midst of such powerful centrifugal forces as suffering and contrast. Schillebeeckx never tires of reminding his readers that Christian praxis is not another form of technical rationality. It is the eschatological proviso, explored here in detail by Hinze, that alone assures the completion of the quest for the *humanum*. But on a more mundane basis, something else is needed to thread together human experience if one is not going to accept the unifying premises of a more symmetrical methodology.

Schillebeeckx finds the answer to this in his giving primacy to the soteriological. In an important way, his whole christological project is about discovering a new soteriology for a postmodern world. The Anselmian model of satisfaction, as venerable as its roots and history may be, does not relate the story of what God has done for us in Jesus adequately for people today. But even more than the need for a new soteriology, Schillebeeckx wishes to give a primacy to the soteriological over the more traditional christological part of the equation of the person and work of Christ.

Such a move is not without its problems or precedents. Emphasis on the soteriological can divorce the significance of Jesus for us from the historical Jesus and reduce that saving meaning to a mere projection of our immediate needs. It can allow for a reduction of the revelatory experience of a saving God to simple human experience, something that happened in nineteenth-century liberal theology and something of which (though generally incorrectly) twentieth-century liberation theologians are accused.

Schillebeeckx eludes these pitfalls, however, through his detailed examination of the historical Jesus and by his critical theory of experience. Schillebeeckx not only affirms the importance of the historical Jesus for his project, he also has done much to restore the life of Jesus to christological awareness. His emphasis on the historical Jesus as an eschatological prophet and his mode of reconstructing the experience of the disciples' growth in resurrection faith assure a solid linkage between the Jesus of history and the Christ of faith. And his critical understanding of the relation of human experience and revelation (explored extensively here by Hilkert) keep him clear of the liberal pitfall.

How does Schillebeeckx then affirm the primacy of the soteriological? It is shaped in many places in his thought by its tie to the prophetic and pneumatic traditions. The need to assert the soteriological dimension of Christology becomes most apparent when the given explanation is found wanting. Then the prophetic and the pneumatic dimensions of the tradition come to rise over the ontological and the dogmatic. Three of the contributions in this volume have explored that move in Schillebeeckx's work: Ross, in Schillebeeckx's understanding of the church; Hines, in his understanding of ministry; and Hinze, in his understanding of eschatology and ethics. In many ways, Schillebeeckx's work in eschatology in the latter half of the 1960s prepared the way for the growing emphasis on the prophetic in the 1970s and 1980s. But he has been making that prophetic dimension a greater part of his preoccupations—so much so that at one point he announced that the projected third volume of the Christology would be on pneumatology. At this point, it would seem that that will not entirely be the case, although pneumatological concerns will weigh heavily in the presentation.

That looking to where the soteriological dimension of God's grace manifests itself in human history is certainly shaping his most recent theology. His search for that saving moment in history has changed his understanding of the church and its ministry. That soteriological interest in its prophetic dimensions portends to change much of the face of Christian theology and of the church if it is followed through. The fact that there is a felt need for that change accounts in some way for the appeal of his writings on Christ, church, and ministry to so many. It is the perceived threat of such a change that alarms others who read those same writings. But in a time when the Eurocentric church becomes a world church, and when the postmodern reality calls for a new and renewed understanding of Christian faith and praxis, must we not run the risk of examining that soteriological dimension more fully, precisely for the sake of fidelity in our discipleship?

THE PRAXIS OF CHRISTIAN EXPERIENCE

Schillebeeckx continues his quest for new ways to help people come to the "point of saying 'yes' to the heart of the gospel." This final chapter has tried to point out some of the foundational dimensions of his thought that guide him in that quest and have made him such an important thinker to so many people, especially in North America, but elsewhere as well. Schillebeeckx remains profoundly concerned with the God bent toward the cause of humanity and with the concrete experiences, sufferings, and hopes of those who would follow after Jesus. He is involved intimately in the praxis of Christian experience. That phrase may seem to be a bit redundant in form, but it captures a number of dimensions of Schillebeeckx's project in being so. Schillebeeckx reminds us often that experience lies at the heart of his theology and that Christian experience is also human experience, not some supranaturalist overlay. And Christian experience is a mutually critical correlation of human experience and Christian tradition, a correlation that finds its expression in a critical Christian praxis of both reflection and action for the sake of the kingdom of God.

WORKS OF EDWARD SCHILLEBEECKX CITED

Christ: The Experience of Jesus as Lord. New York: Crossroad, 1980.

Christ the Sacrament of the Encounter with God. New York: Sheed and Ward, 1963.

On Christian Faith: The Spiritual, Ethical and Political Dimensions. New York: Crossroad, 1987.

"The Christian Community and its Office Bearers," *Concilium* 133 (1980): 95–133.

The Church with a Human Face: A New and Expanded Theology of Ministry. New York: Crossroad, 1985.

"Critical Theories and Christian Political Commitment," *Concilium* 84 (1973): 48–61.

The Eucharist. New York: Sheed and Ward, 1968.

God Among Us: The Gospel Proclaimed. New York: Crossroad, 1983.

God Is New Each Moment: Edward Schillebeeckx in Conversation with Huub Oosterhuis and Piet Hoogeveen. New York: Seabury, 1983.

God the Future of Man. New York: Sheed and Ward, 1968.

Interim Report on the Books "Jesus" and "Christ." New York: Crossroad, 1980.

Jesus: An Experiment in Christology. New York: Seabury, 1979.

Marriage: Human Reality and Saving Mystery. New York: Sheed and Ward, 1966.

Ministry: Leadership in the Community of Jesus Christ. New York: Crossroad, 1981.

The Schillebeeckx Case. Edited by Ted Schoof. New York: Paulist Press, 1984.

The Schillebeeckx Reader. Edited by Robert J. Schreiter. New York: Crossroad, 1984.

The Understanding of Faith. New York: Seabury, 1974.

World and Church. New York: Sheed and Ward, 1971.

Notes on Contributors

Janet M. Callewaert is Assistant Professor of Religious Studies at Clarke College. She previously served for two years as Lecturer in the Department of Religious Studies at the Catholic University of America, where she completed a Ph.D. in religious studies on the soteriology of Edward Schillebeeckx.

John P. Galvin is Associate Professor of Systematic Theology at the Catholic University of America. He is a priest of the Archdiocese of Boston. He received his doctorate from the University of Innsbruck and taught systematic theology at St. John's Seminary from 1970 to 1987. He has contributed to *A World of Grace: An Introduction to the Themes and Foundations of Karl Rahner's Theology* and numerous theological journals in North America and Europe.

Donald J. Goergen, O.P., is presently Provincial of the Central Dominican Province in the United States. He has a doctorate from the Aquinas Institute of Theology, where he taught for ten years. Among his published works are *The Sexual Celibate, The Power of Love,* and *The Mission and Ministry of Jesus,* the first of a projected five-volume theology of Jesus.

Mary Catherine Hilkert, O.P., is Assistant Professor of Systematic Theology at the Aquinas Institute of Theology. She received her doctorate from the Catholic University of America with a dissertation on Schillebeeckx's hermeneutics of tradition as a basis for a theology of proclamation. She has published articles on Schillebeeckx's theology in *U.S. Dominican* and *The Thomist* and is presently serving on the Board of Directors of the Catholic Theological Society of America.

William J. Hill, O.P., is Professor Emeritus at the Catholic University of America. He received his doctorate from the University of Saint Thomas in Rome and taught theology for thirty-five years. His published works include *Knowing the Unknown God* and *The Three-Personed God*, as well as numerous articles. He is former editor of *The Thomist* and a past president of the Catholic Theological Society of America.

Mary E. Hines, S.N.D., is Assistant Professor in the Department of Sacramental/Ecclesial/Liturgical Theology at the Washington Theological Union. She received a doctorate in systematic theology from the University of St. Michael's College in Toronto. She regularly teaches courses in the theology of ministry and has published several articles.

Bradford E. Hinze is Assistant Professor of Systematic Theology at Marquette University. He received his doctorate in Christian theology from the University of Chicago. He specializes in nineteenth- and twentieth-century theologies.

William L. Portier is Associate Professor of Theology at Mount Saint Mary's College in Emmitsburg, Maryland. He received his doctorate from the University of Saint Michael's College in Toronto. He is the author of *Isaac Hecker and the First Vatican Council* and articles in several U.S. and Canadian theological journals. In 1986 he was elected vice president of the College Theology Society. He has special research interests in the work of Edward Schillebeeckx and is preparing a biography of John R. Slattery.

Susan A. Ross is Assistant Professor of Theology at Loyola University of Chicago. She received her doctorate in Christian theology from the University of Chicago and has taught at Saint Norbert College and Duquesne University. She has published a number of articles and is currently engaged in research on the role of the body and nature in feminist and sacramental theology.

Robert J. Schreiter, C.PP.S., is Professor of Doctrinal Theology at the Catholic Theological Union in Chicago. He received his doctorate under the direction of Edward Schillebeeckx at the University of Nijmegen in the Netherlands. His works include *The Schillebeeckx Reader, Contructing Local Theologies,* and a number of articles on Edward Schillebeeckx and other subjects. He is editor of *New Theology Review.*

Index